Tender is the Light

To Valentine,
my love and my light.

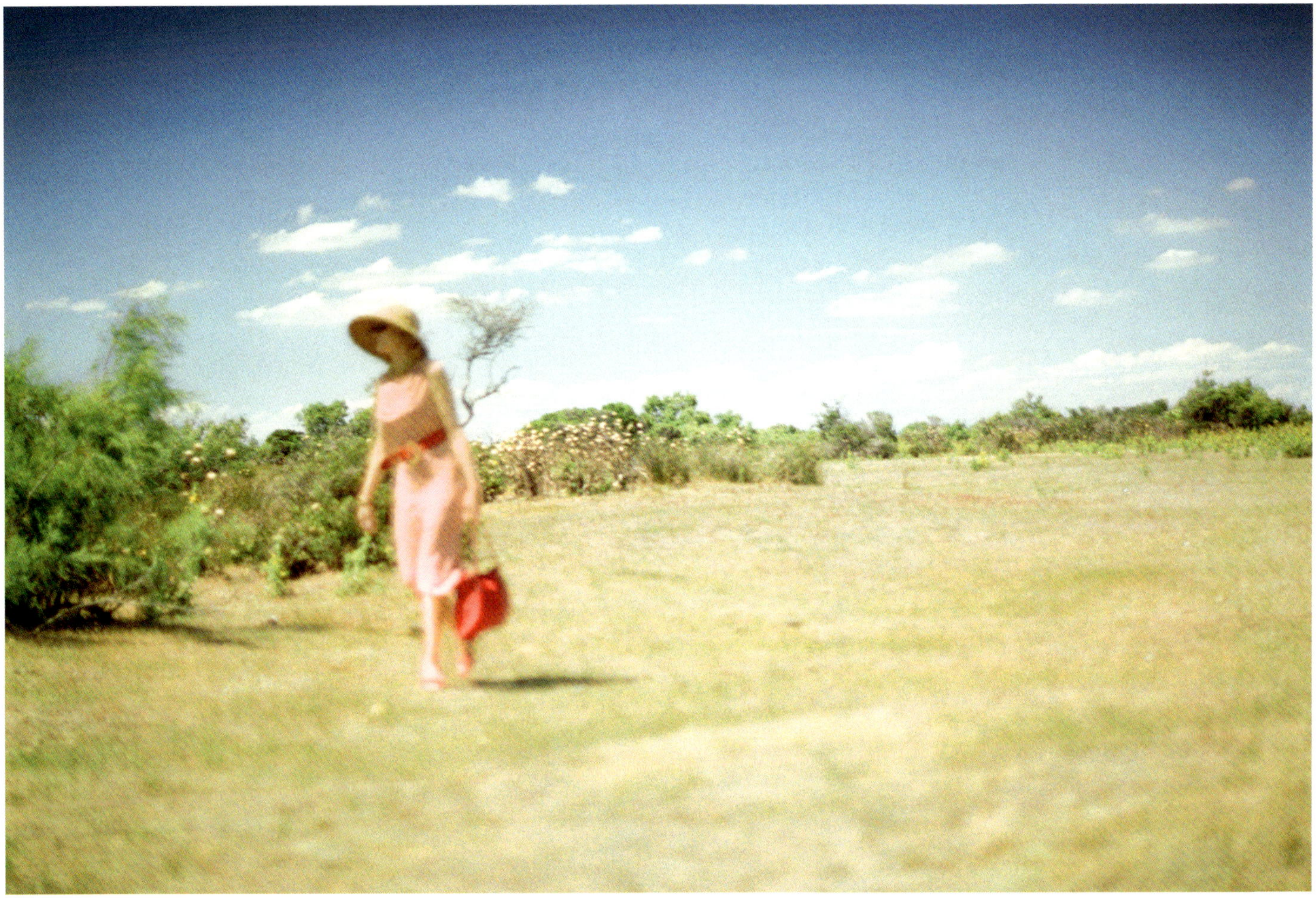

David Julian Leonard

\

tender is the light

KEHRER

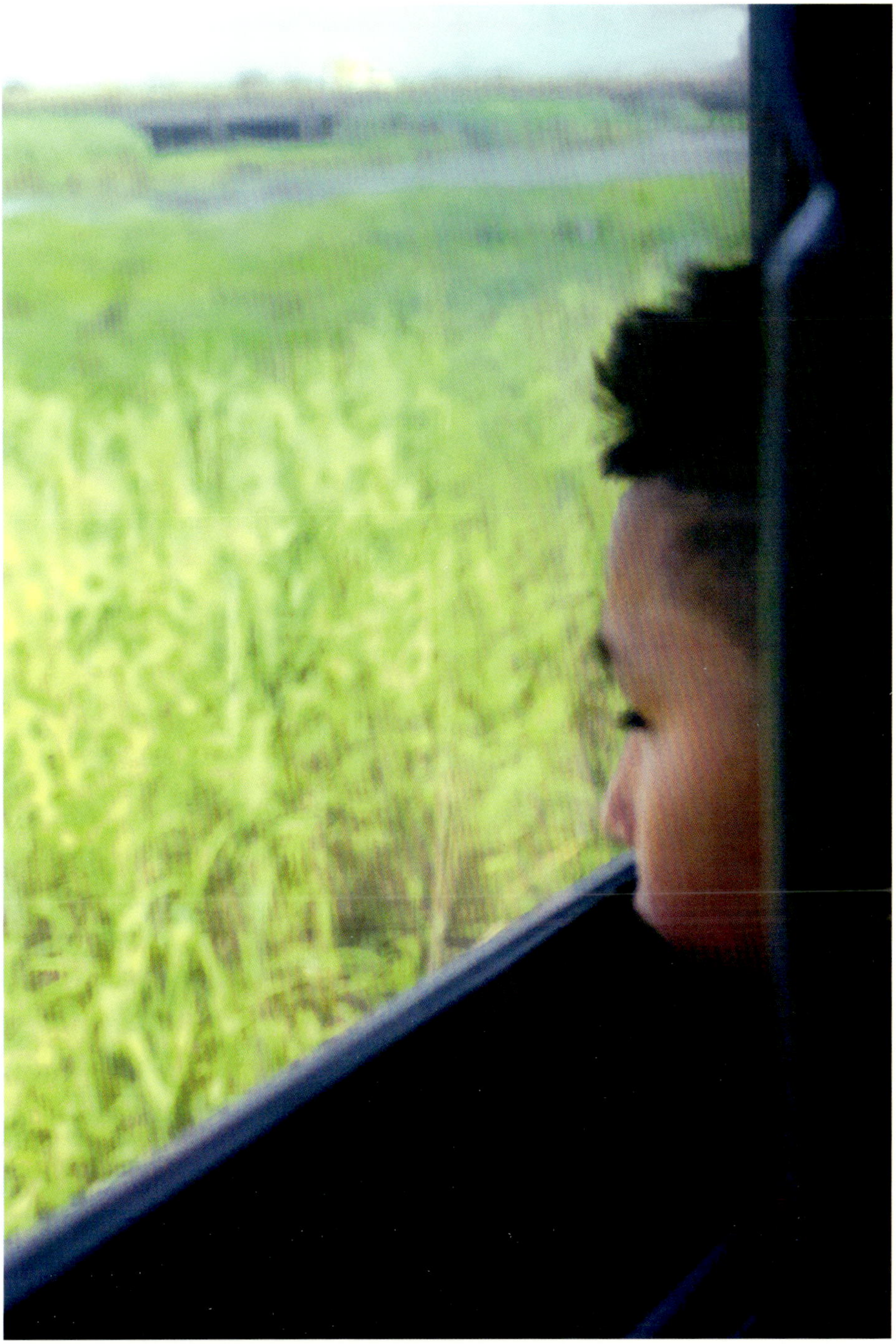

TRAIN APPROACHING

\

New Orleans – 2011

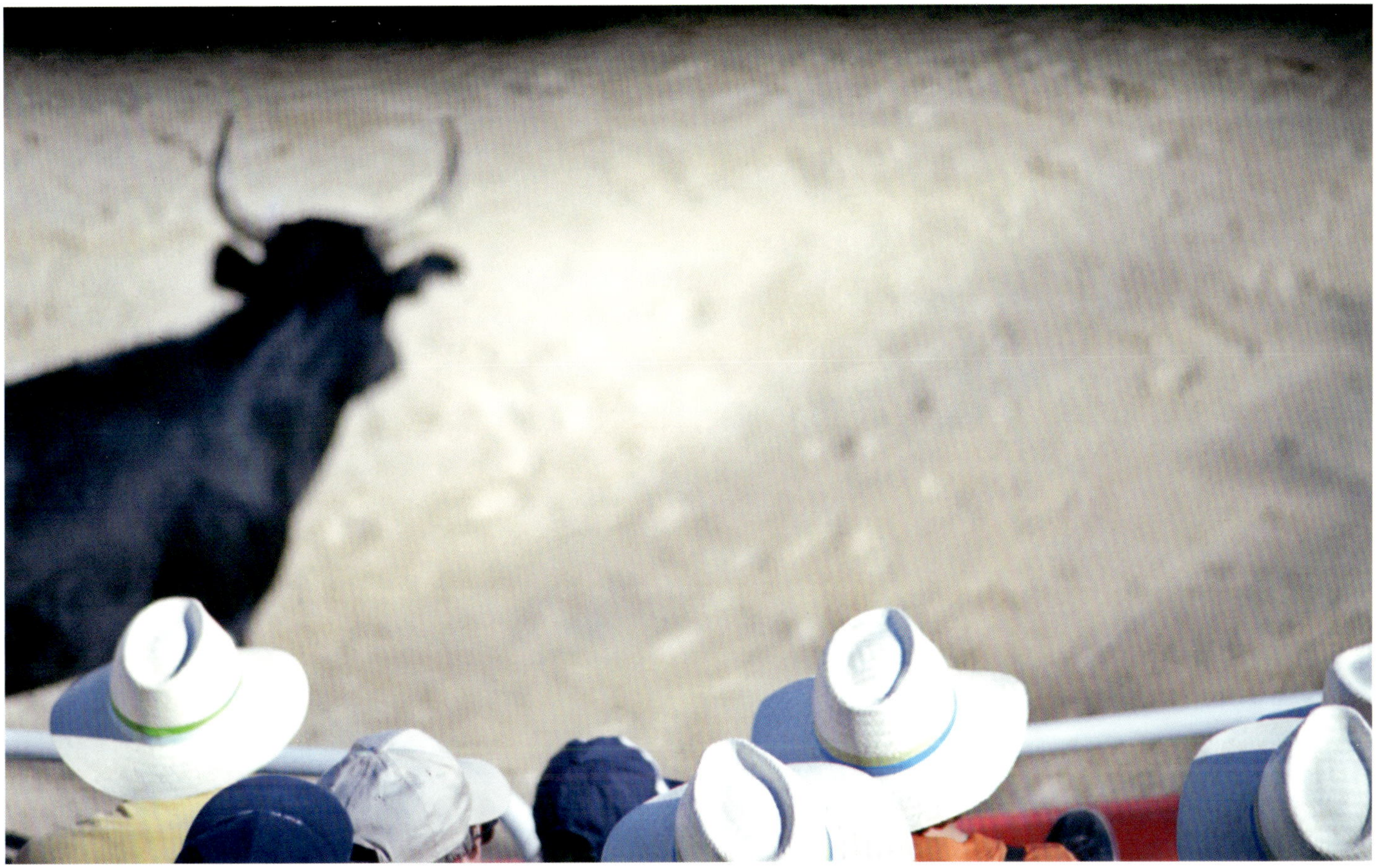

LA CORRIDA
\
Arles – 2002

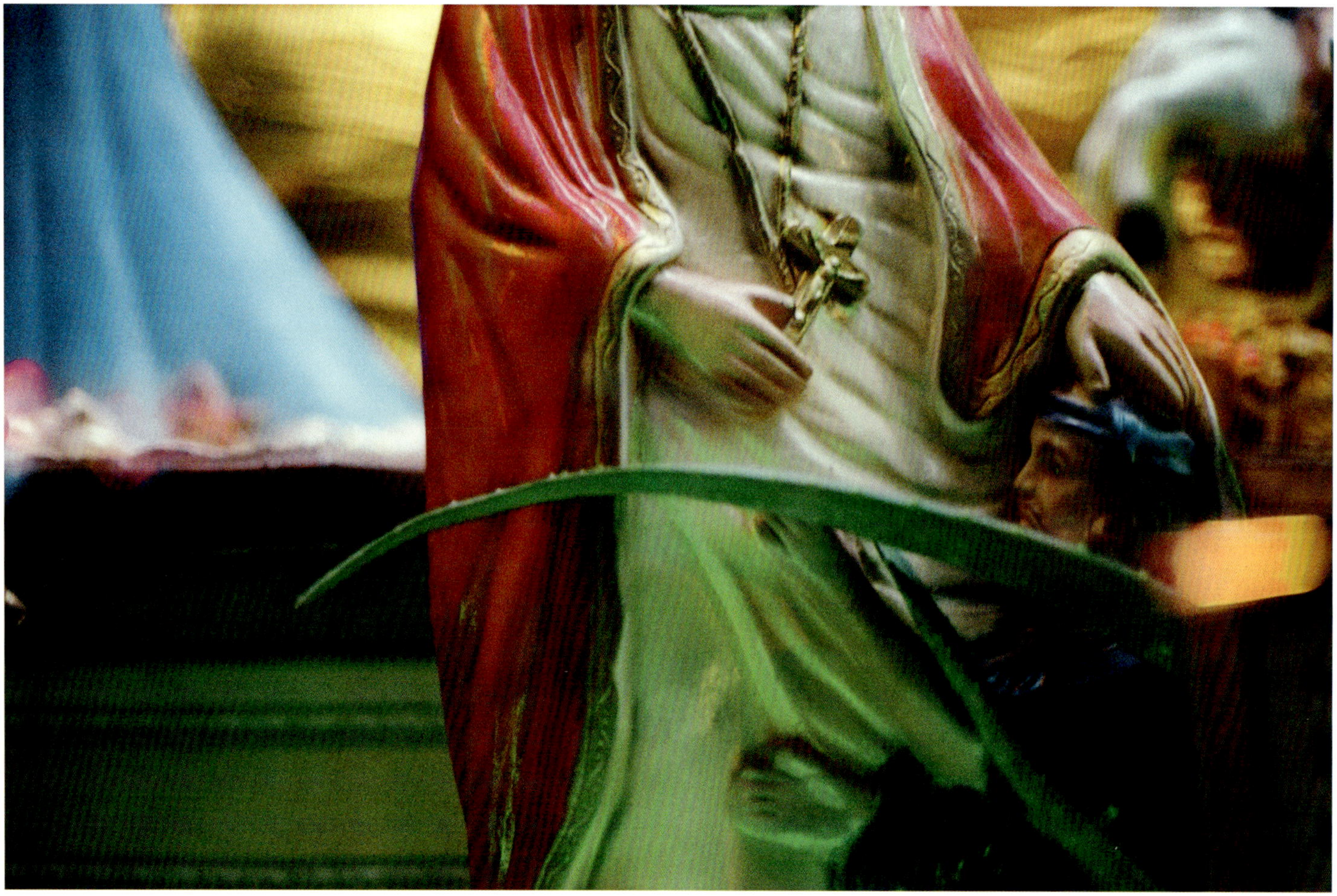

STORE WINDOW
\
5th Avenue, Brooklyn – 2000

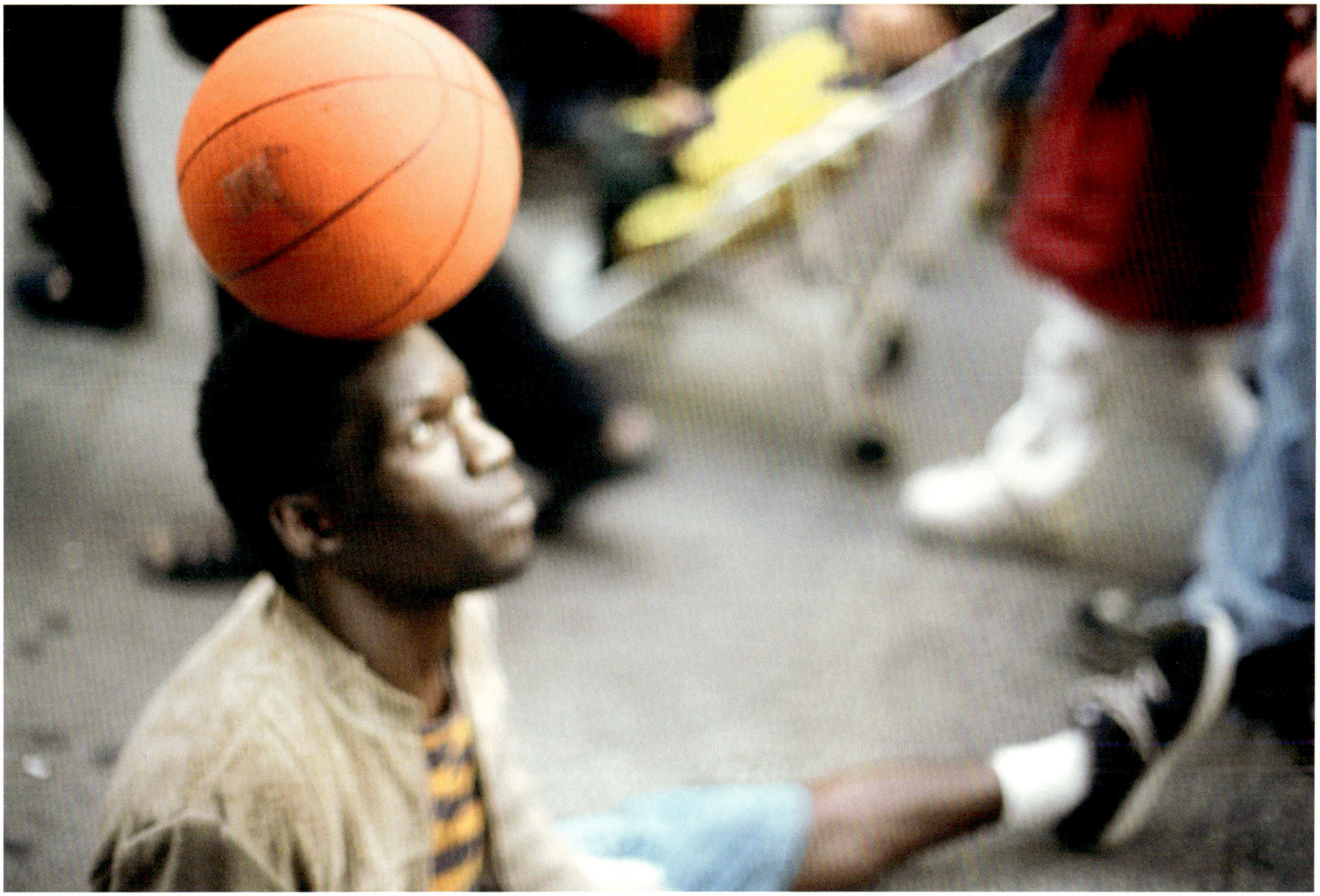

STREET PERFORMER

\

Times Square, Manhattan – 1999

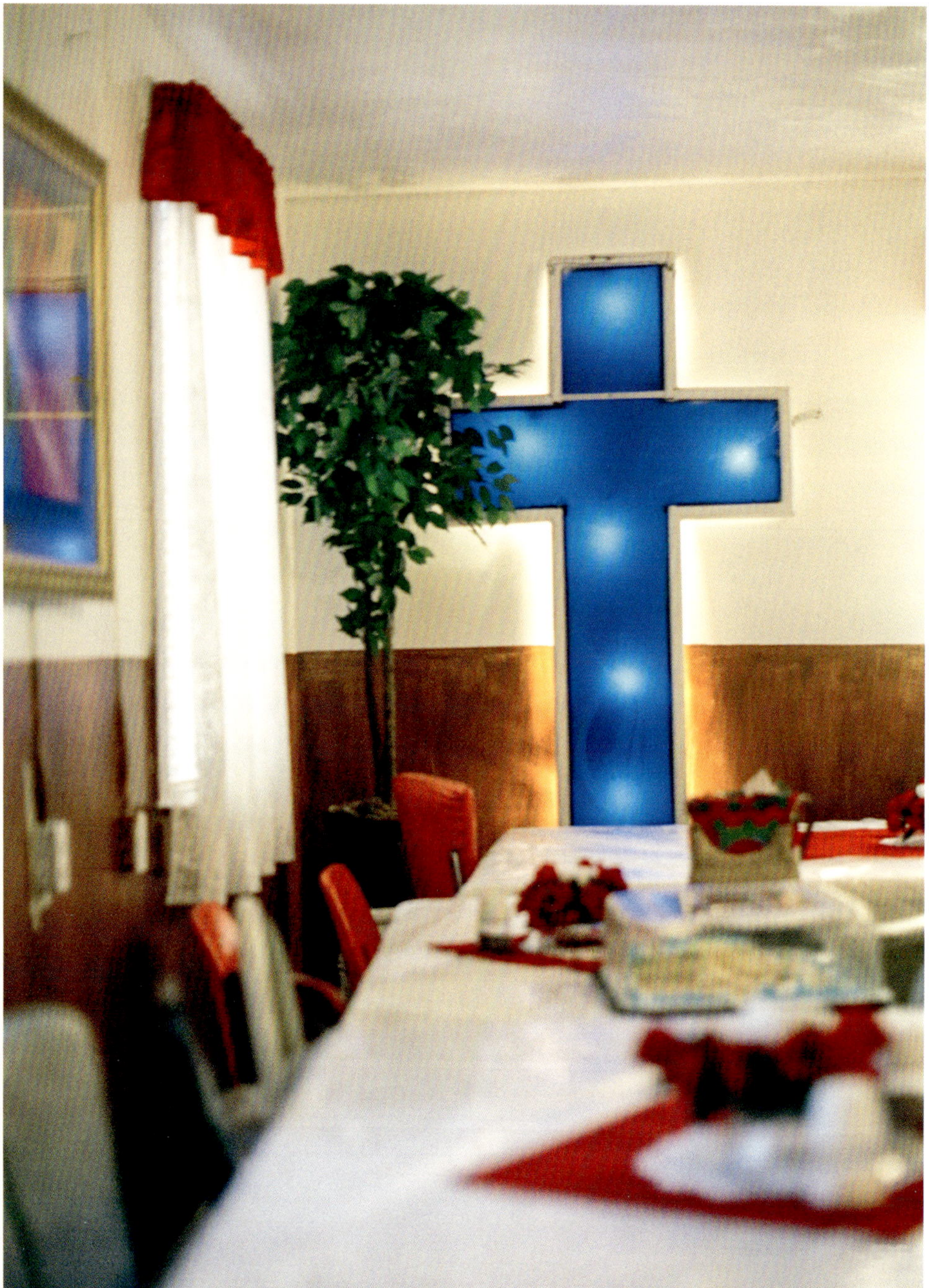

CHURCH (BACKSTAGE)

\

Memphis – 2002

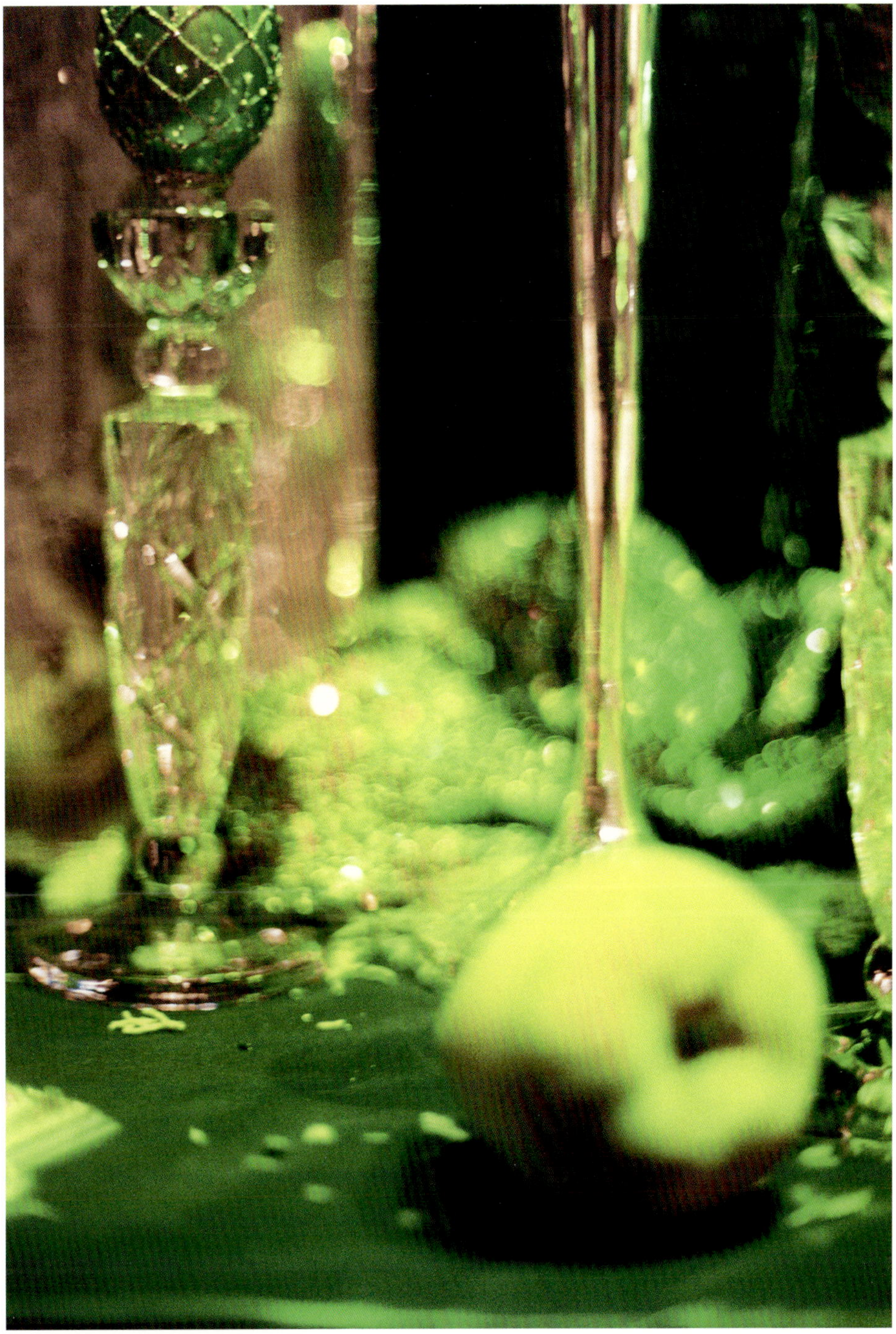

STORE WINDOW
\
5th Avenue, Manhattan – 2000

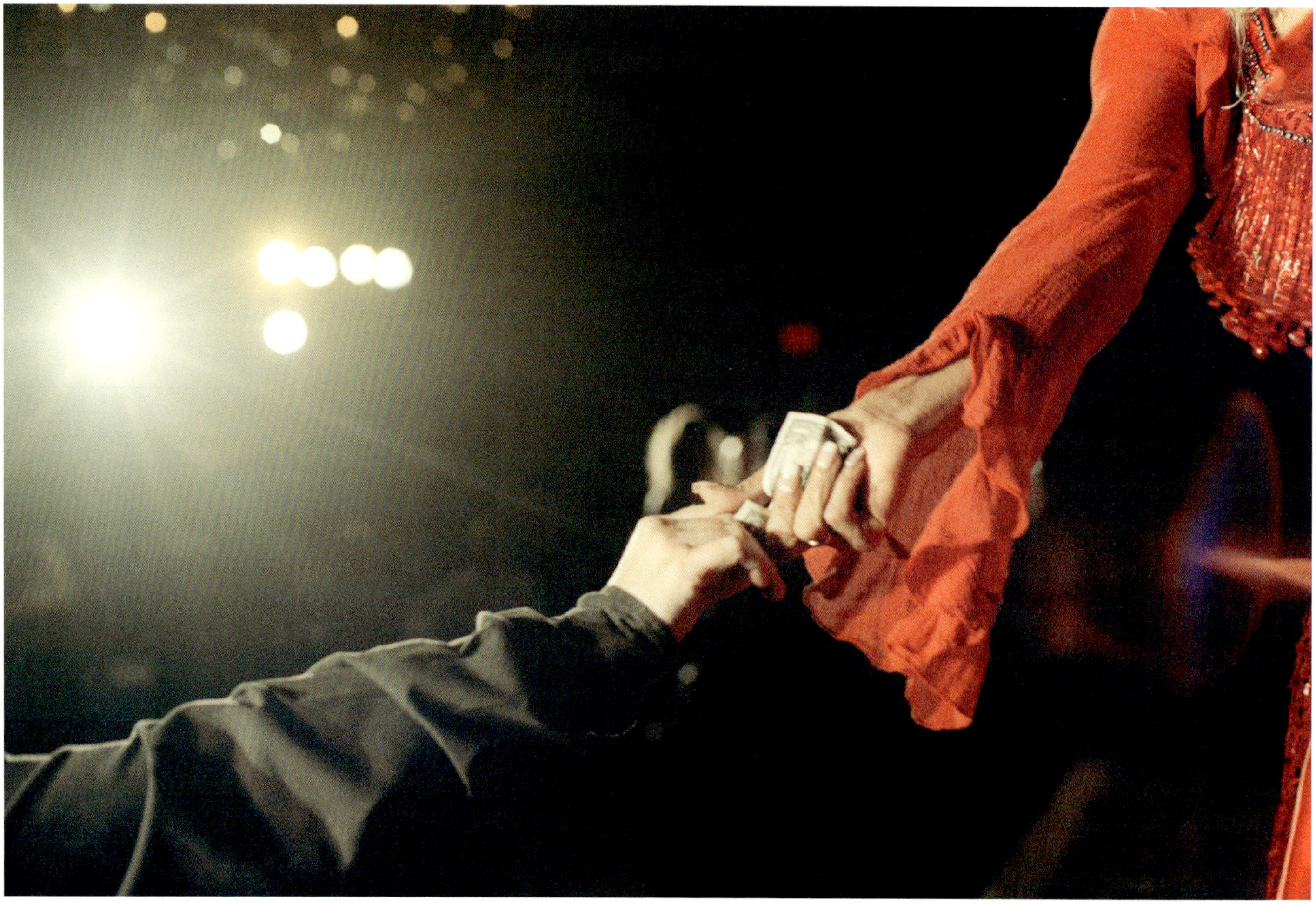

MISS GAY AMERICA PAGEANT

\

Memphis – 2007

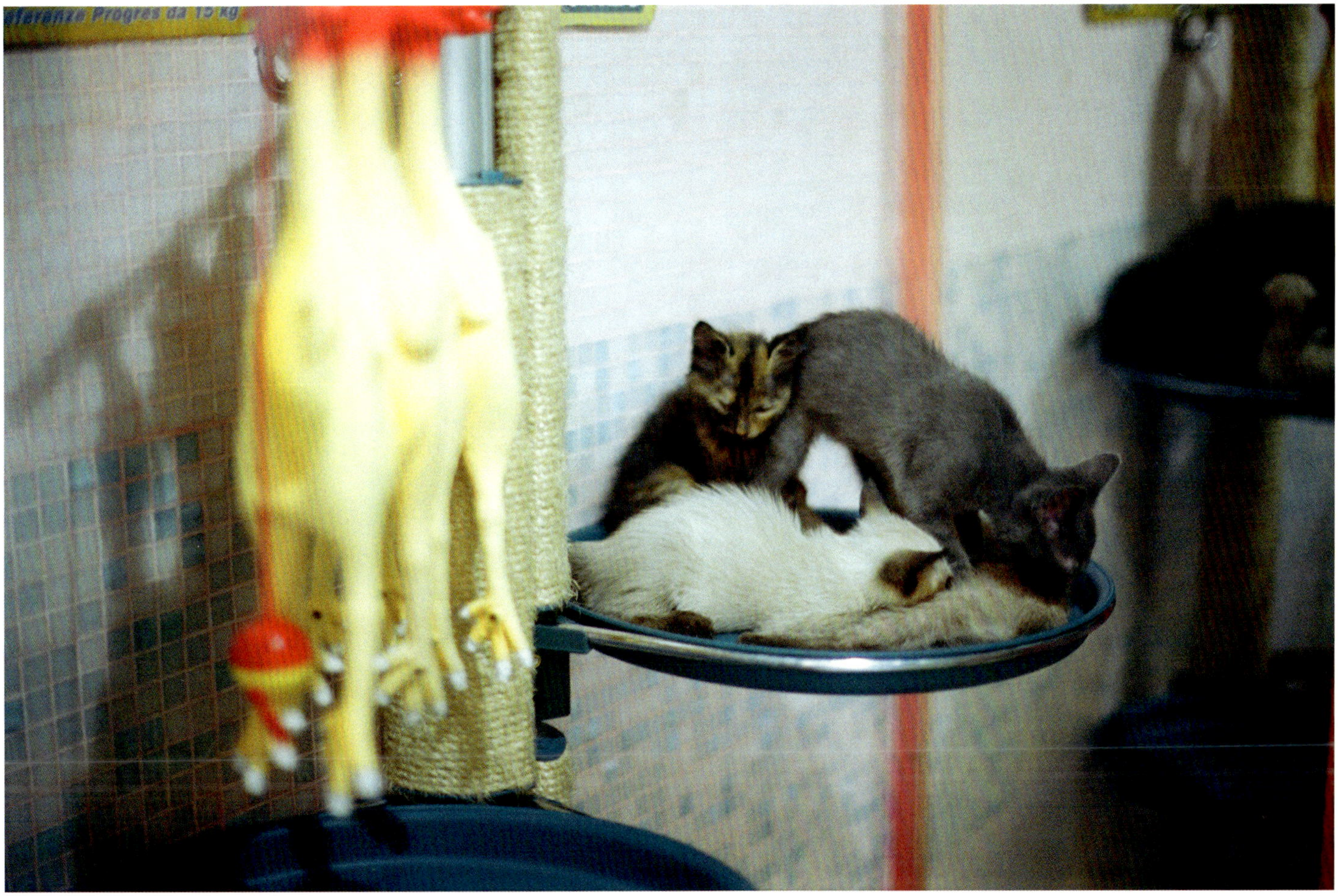

STORE WINDOW

\

Città di Castello, Italy – 2003

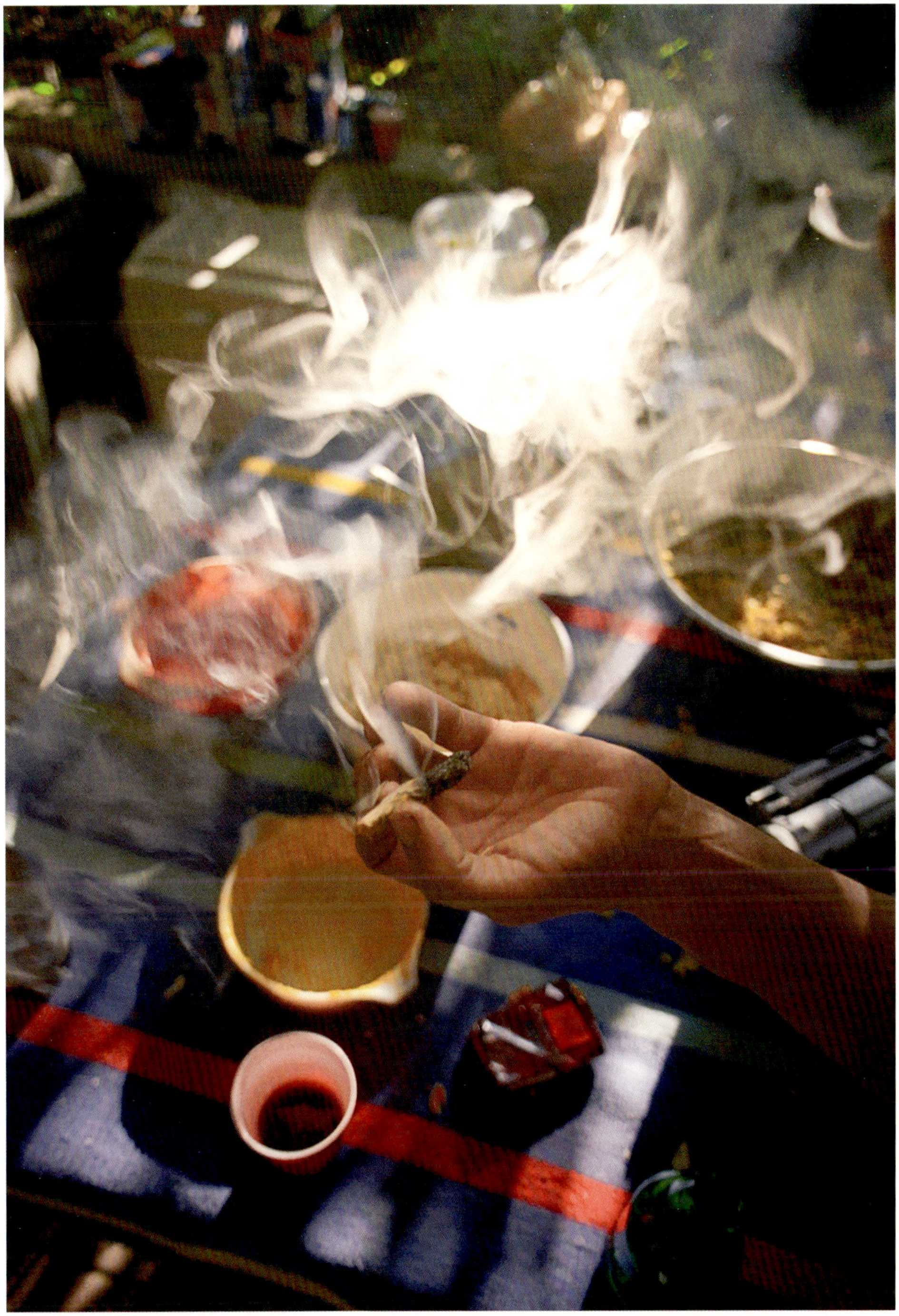

I'D TELL YOU BUT I'D HAVE TO KILL YOU

\

Memphis – 2000

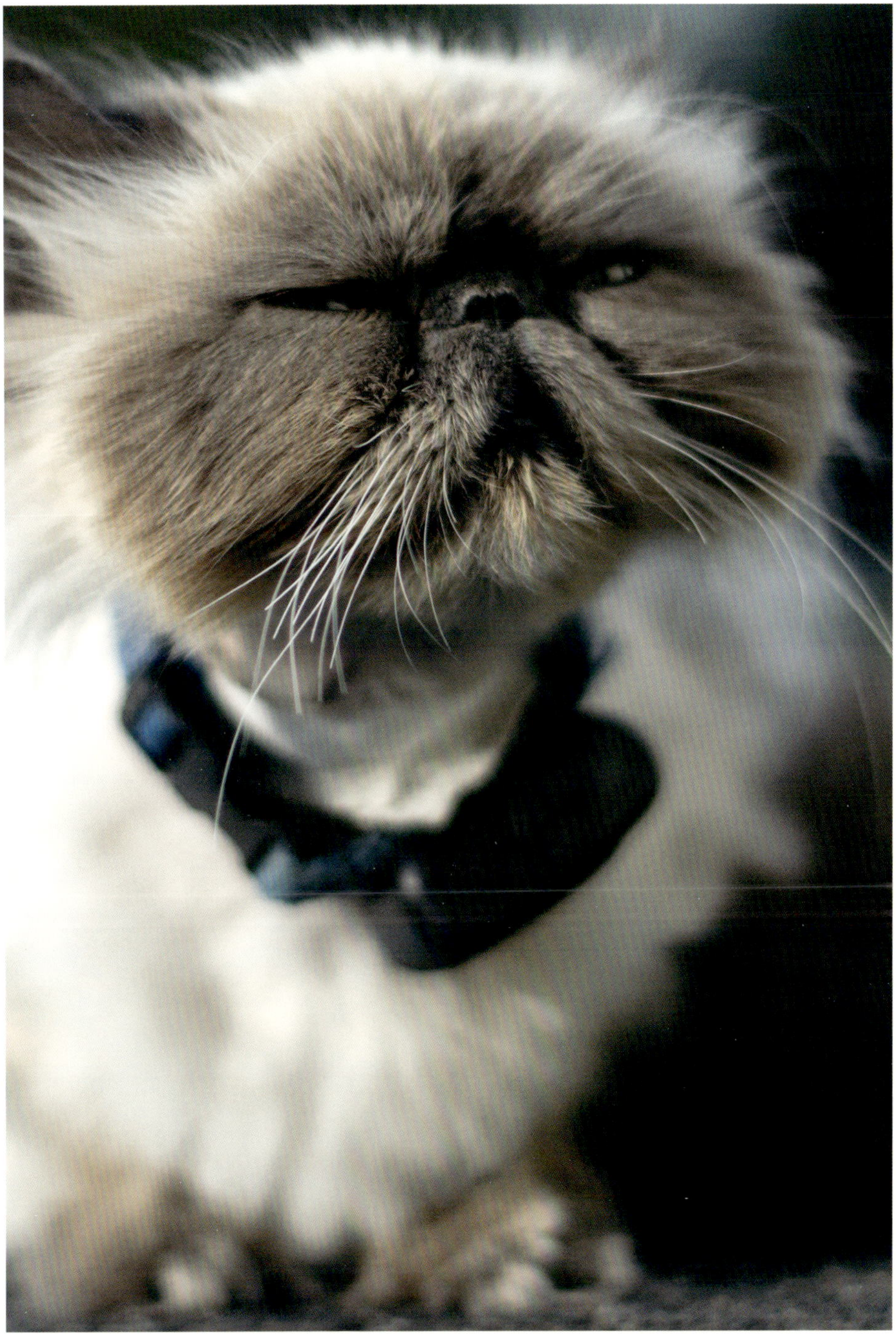

STEPHEN SHORE'S CAT

\

Hudson Valley, NY – 2012

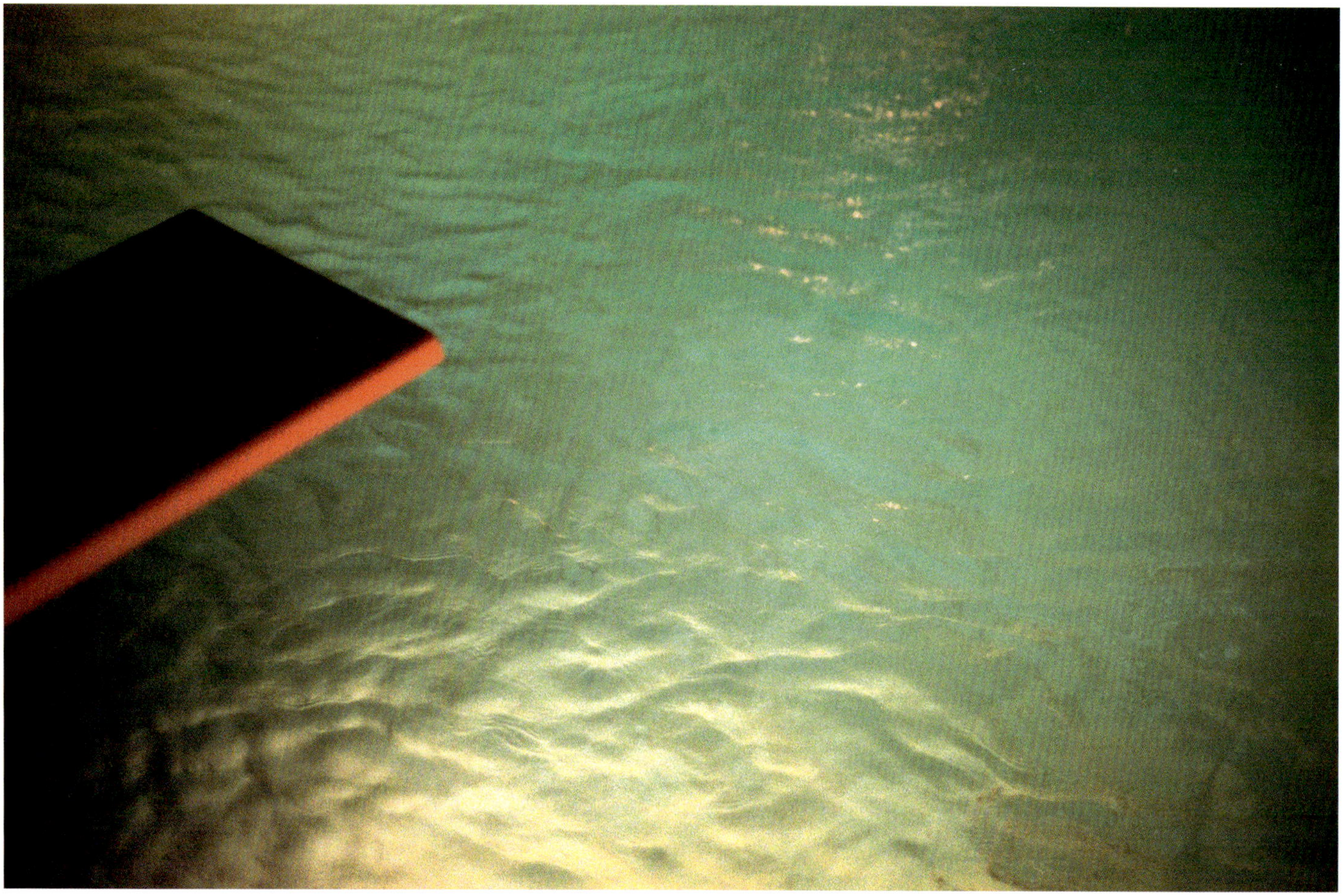

POOL WATER
\
Memphis – 2000

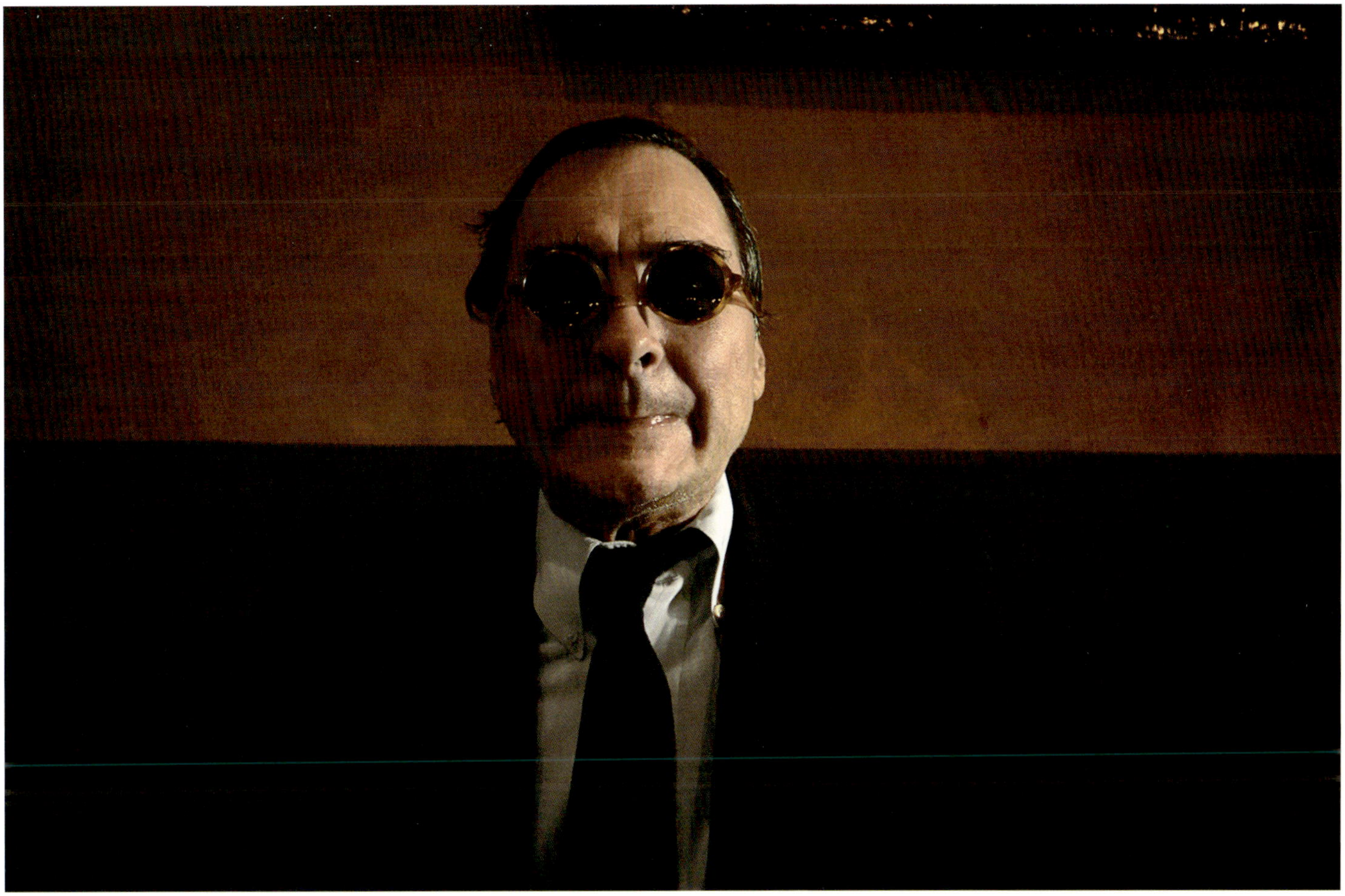

WILLIAM EGGLESTON

\

Santa Monica, California – 1997

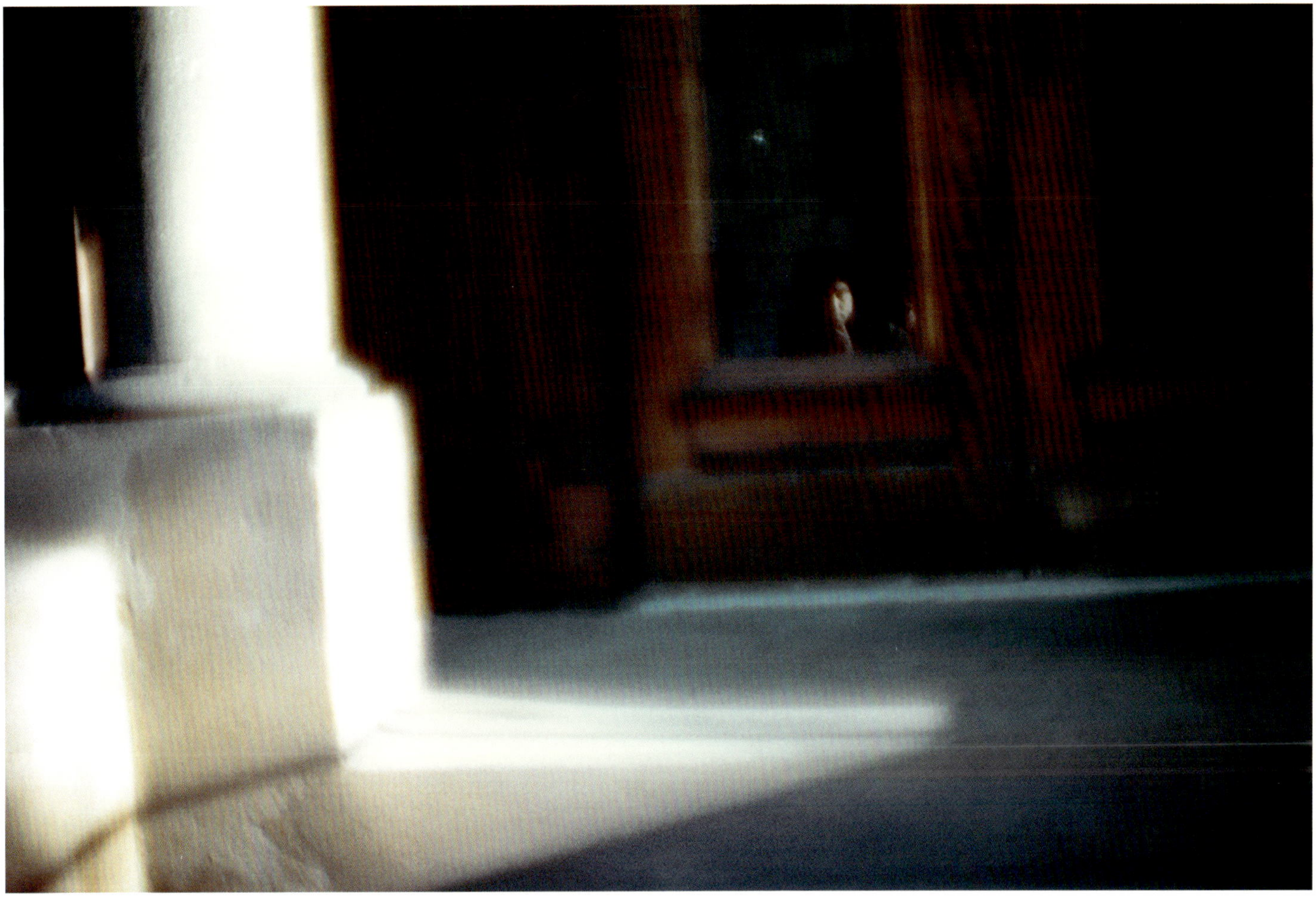

SELF PORTRAIT AFTER HOPPER
\
Brooklyn – 2000

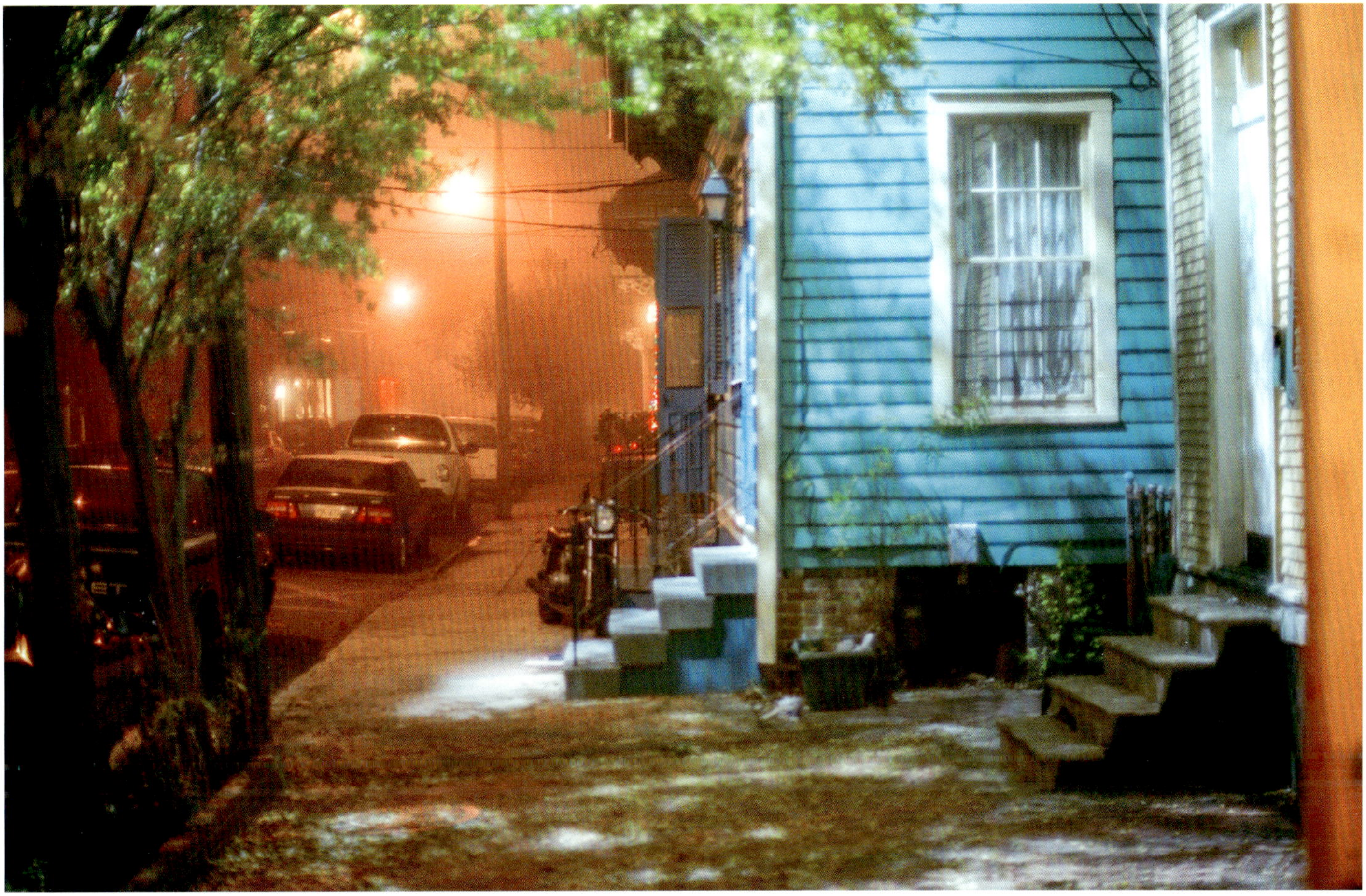

FOG IN THE FAUBOURG MARIGNY

\

New Orleans – 2007

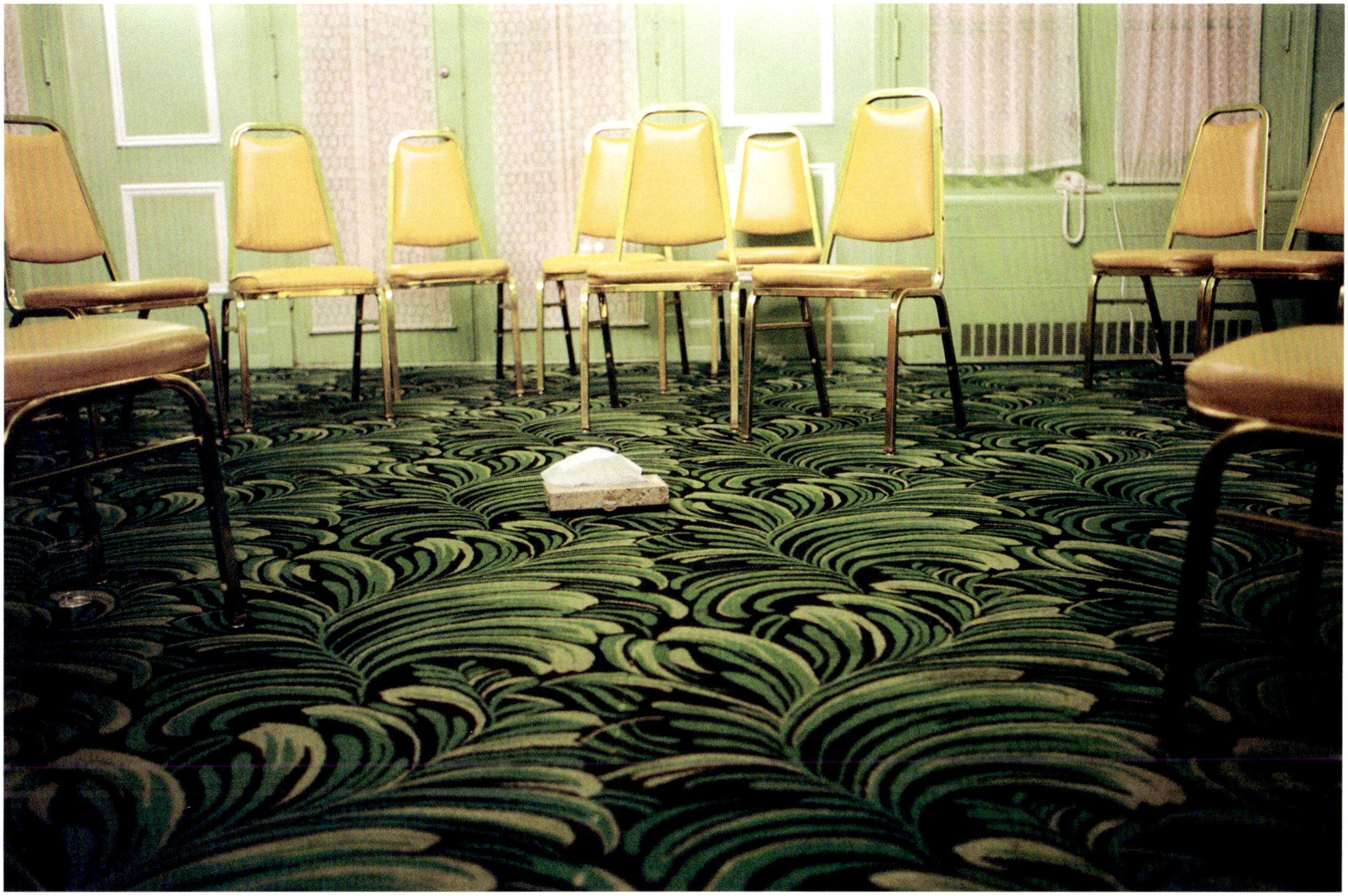

KLEENEX BOX

\

Hot Springs, Arkansas – 2003

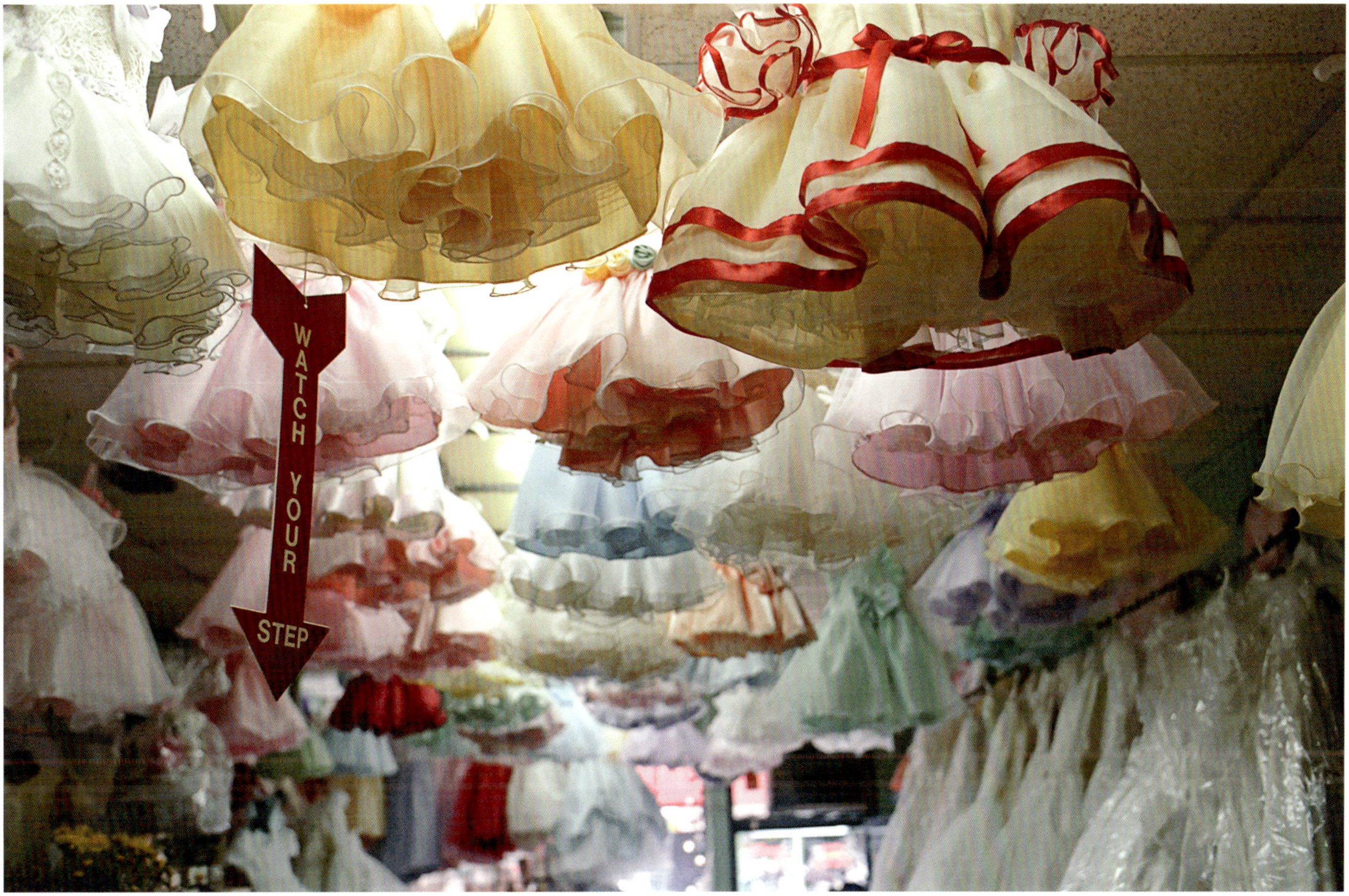

DRESSES

\

Brooklyn – 2002

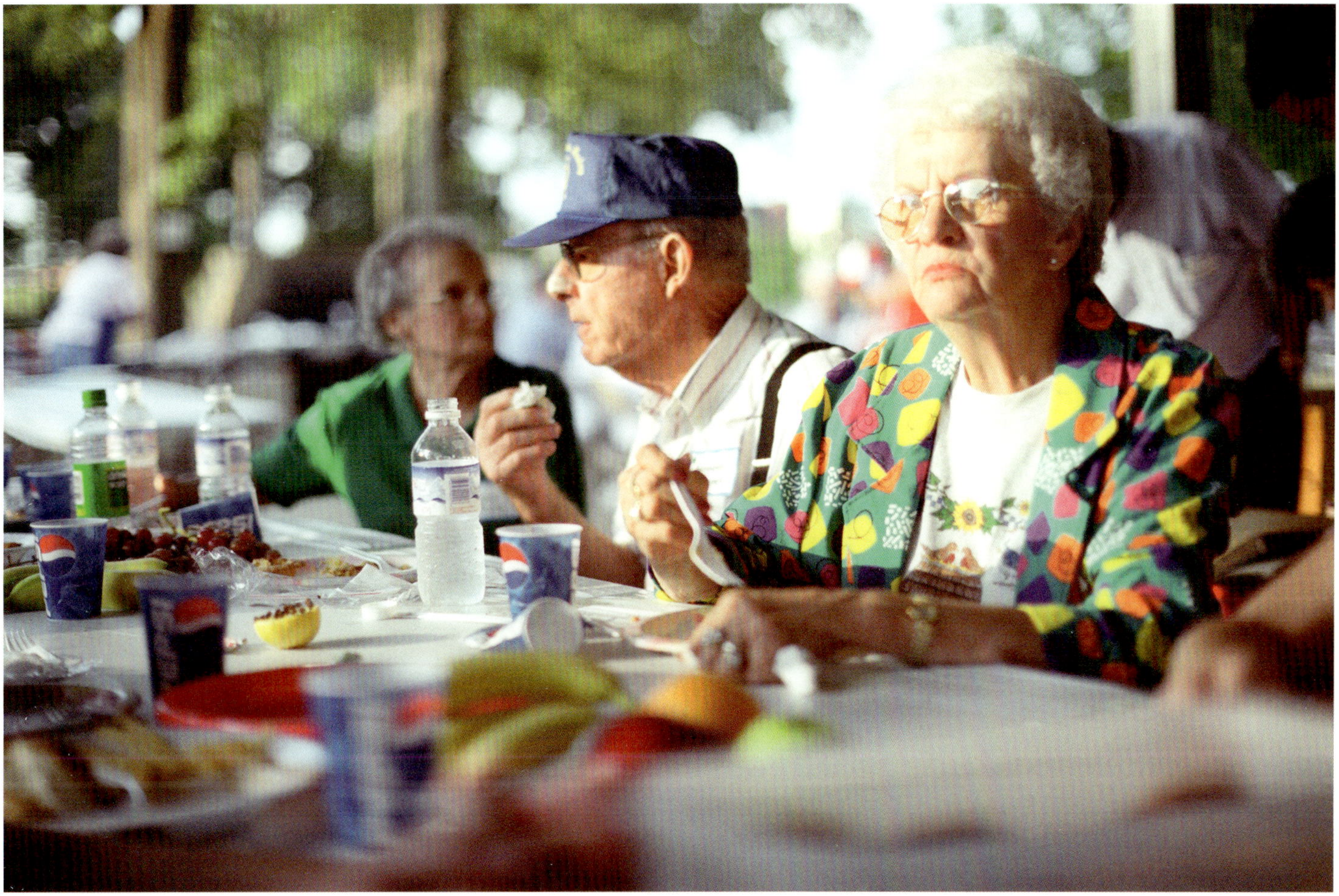

FAMILY REUNION

\

Mississippi – 1999

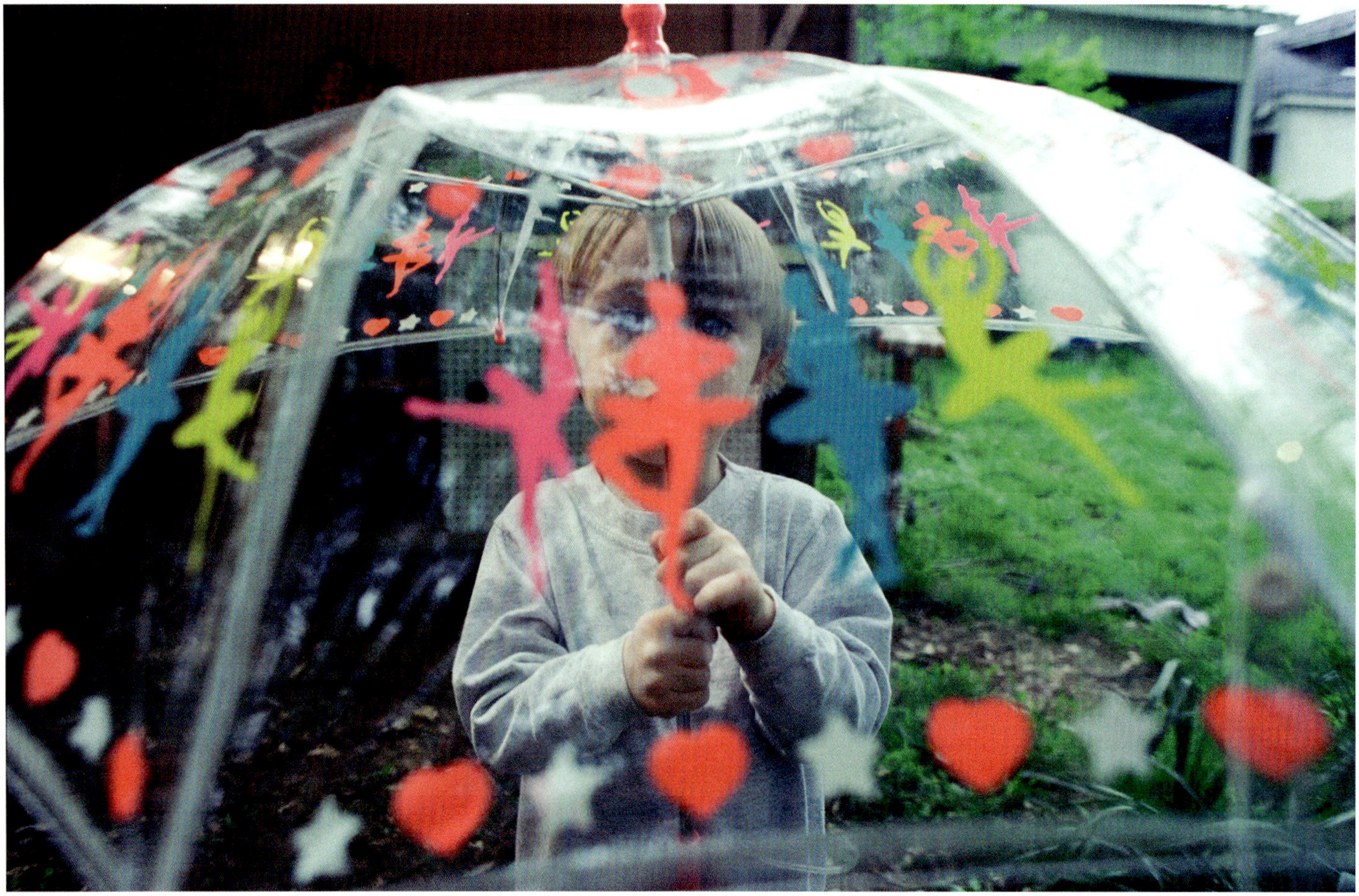

PHINEAS' RAINBOW
\
Memphis – 2001

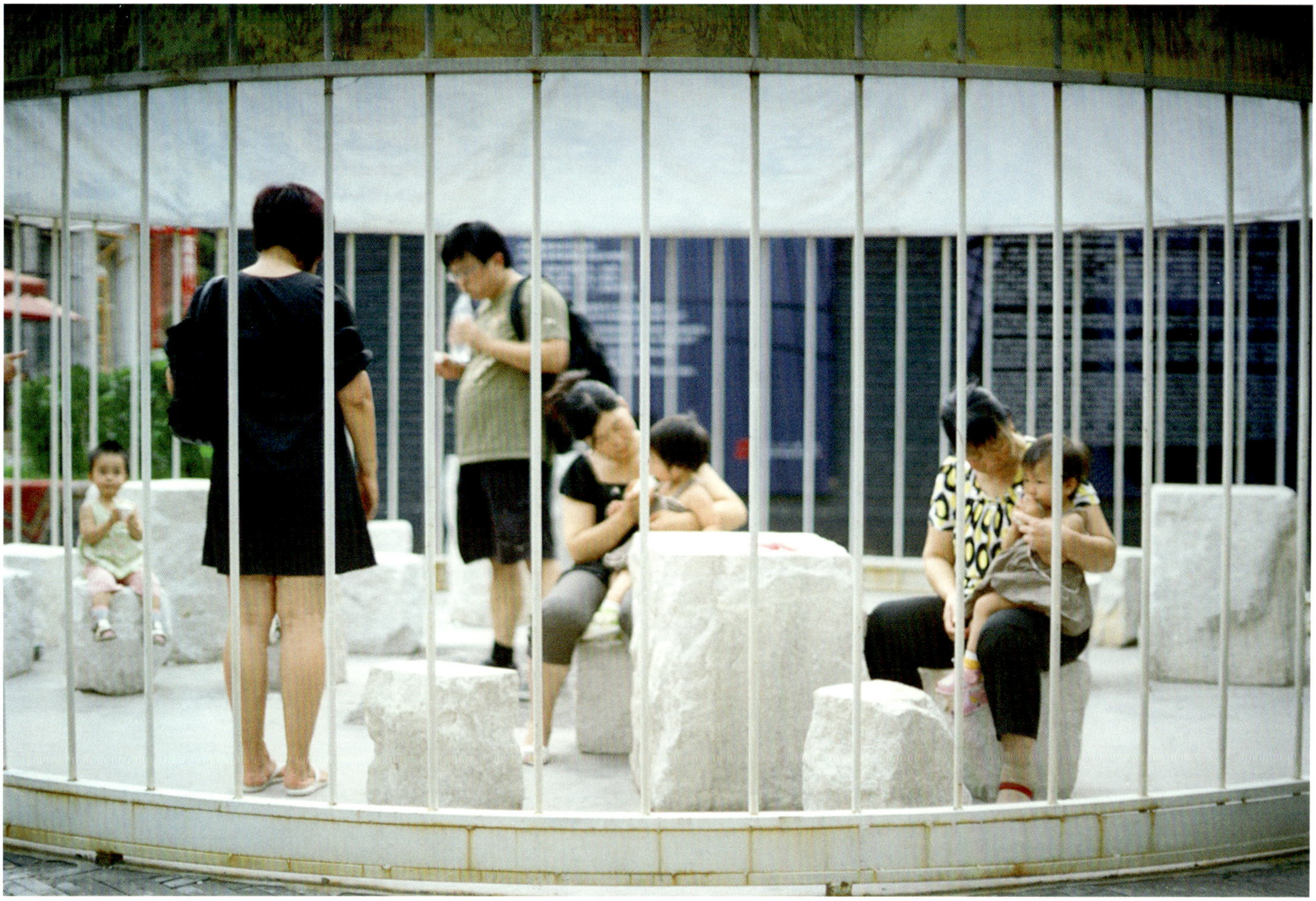

DON'T FEED THE HUMANS
\
Beijing – 2009

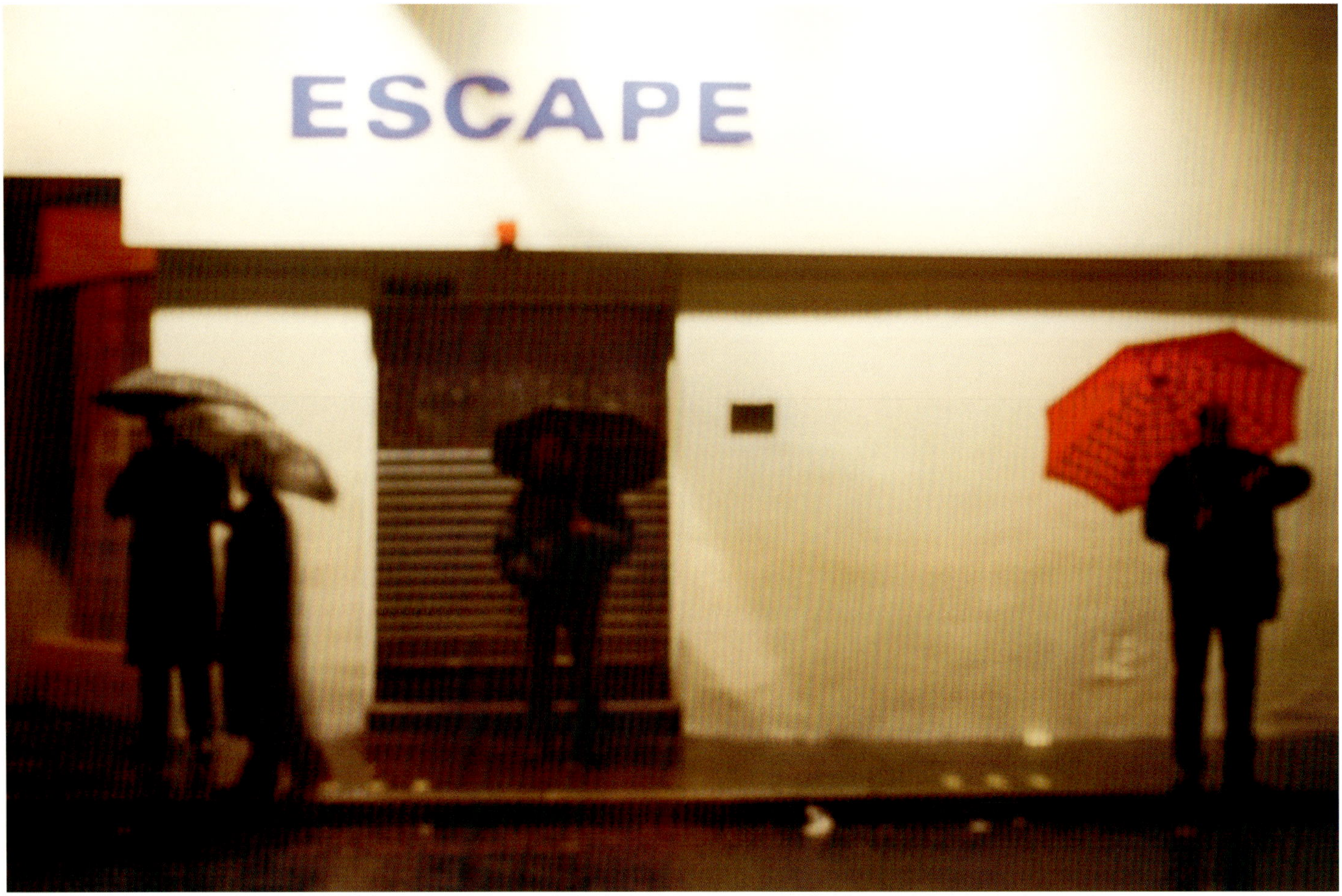

ESCAPE
\
Soho, London – 1997

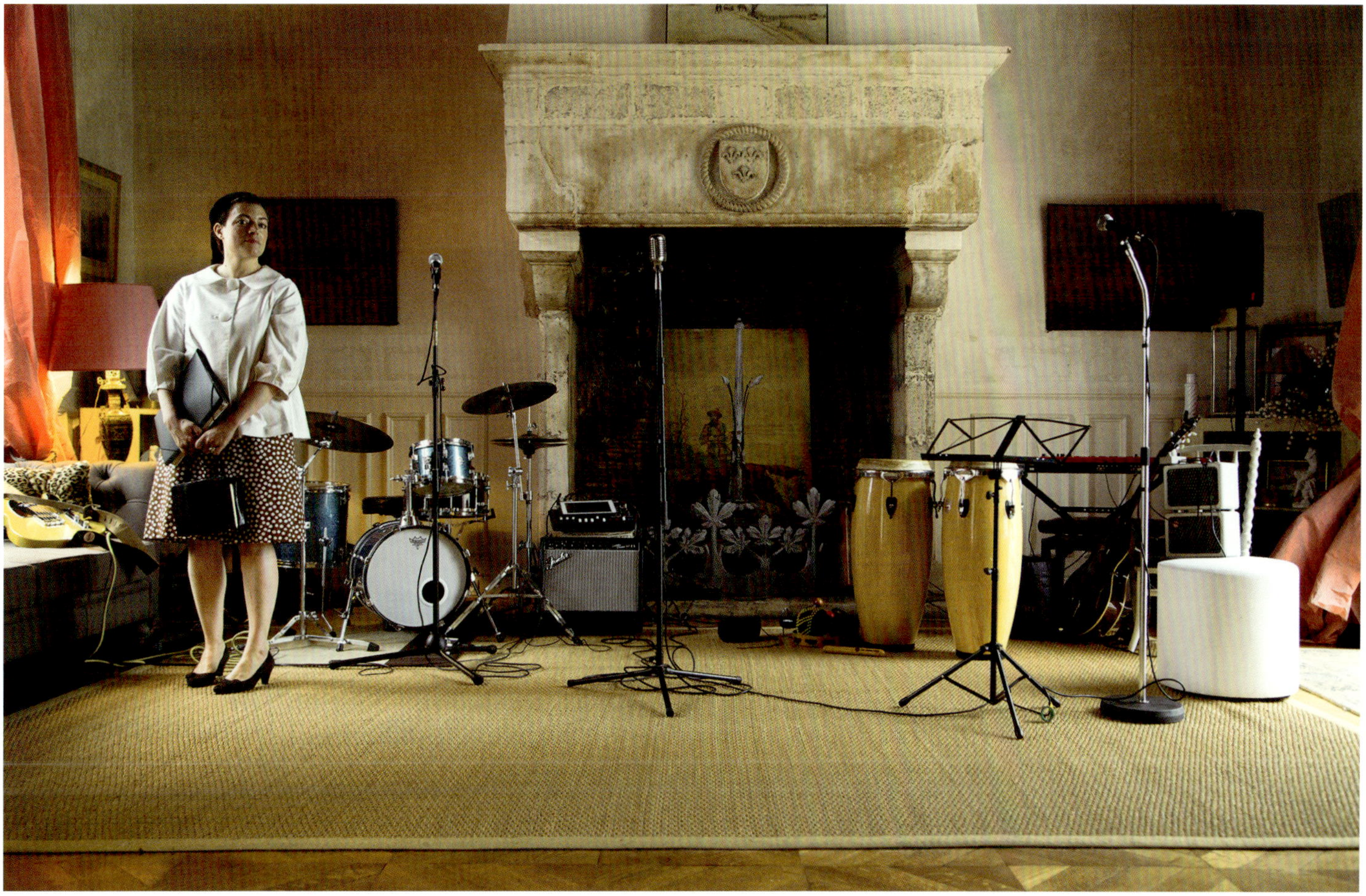

OPERA SINGER

\

Senlis, France – 2014

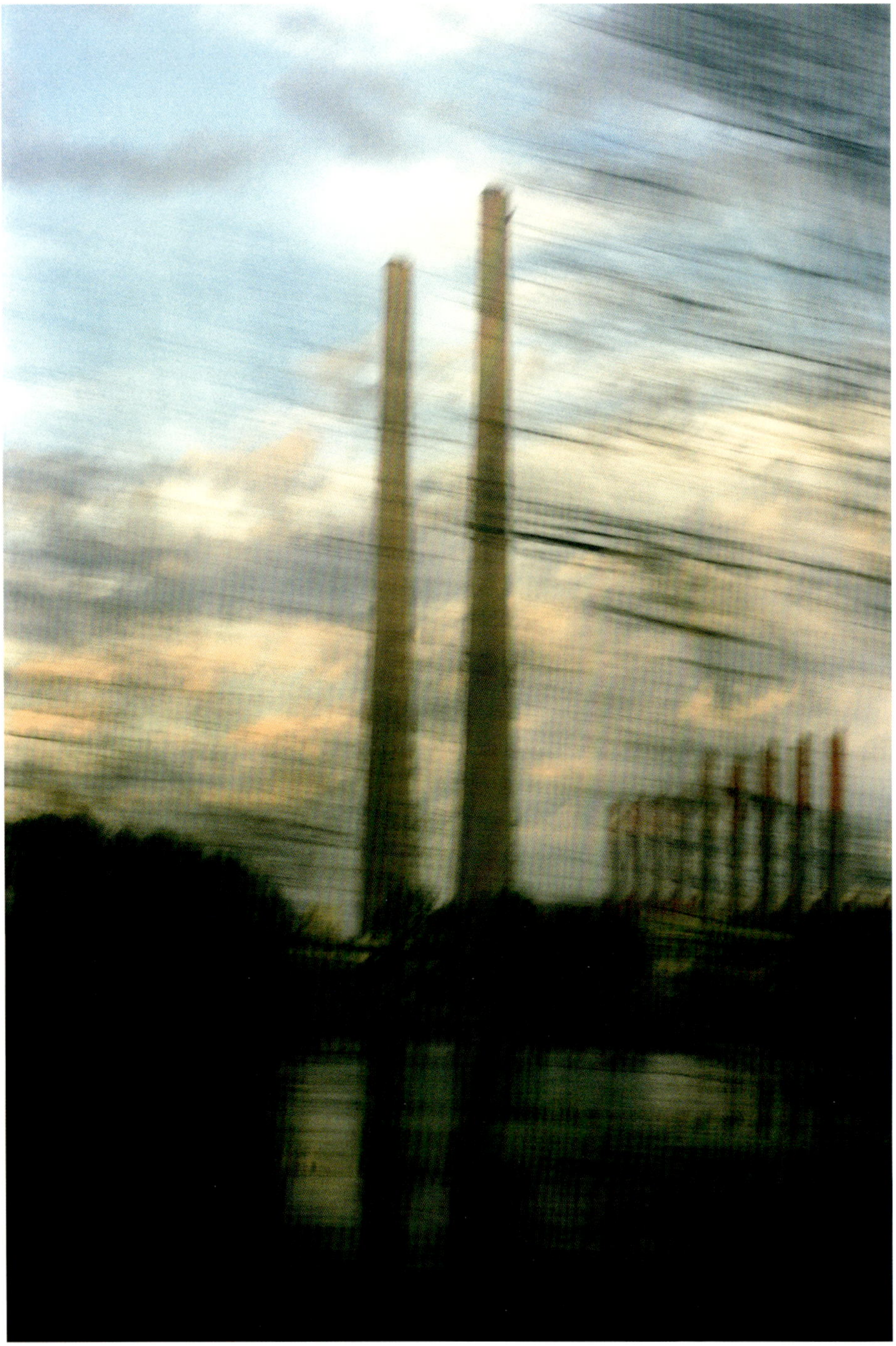

T.V.A. TOWERS

\

Tennessee – 2001

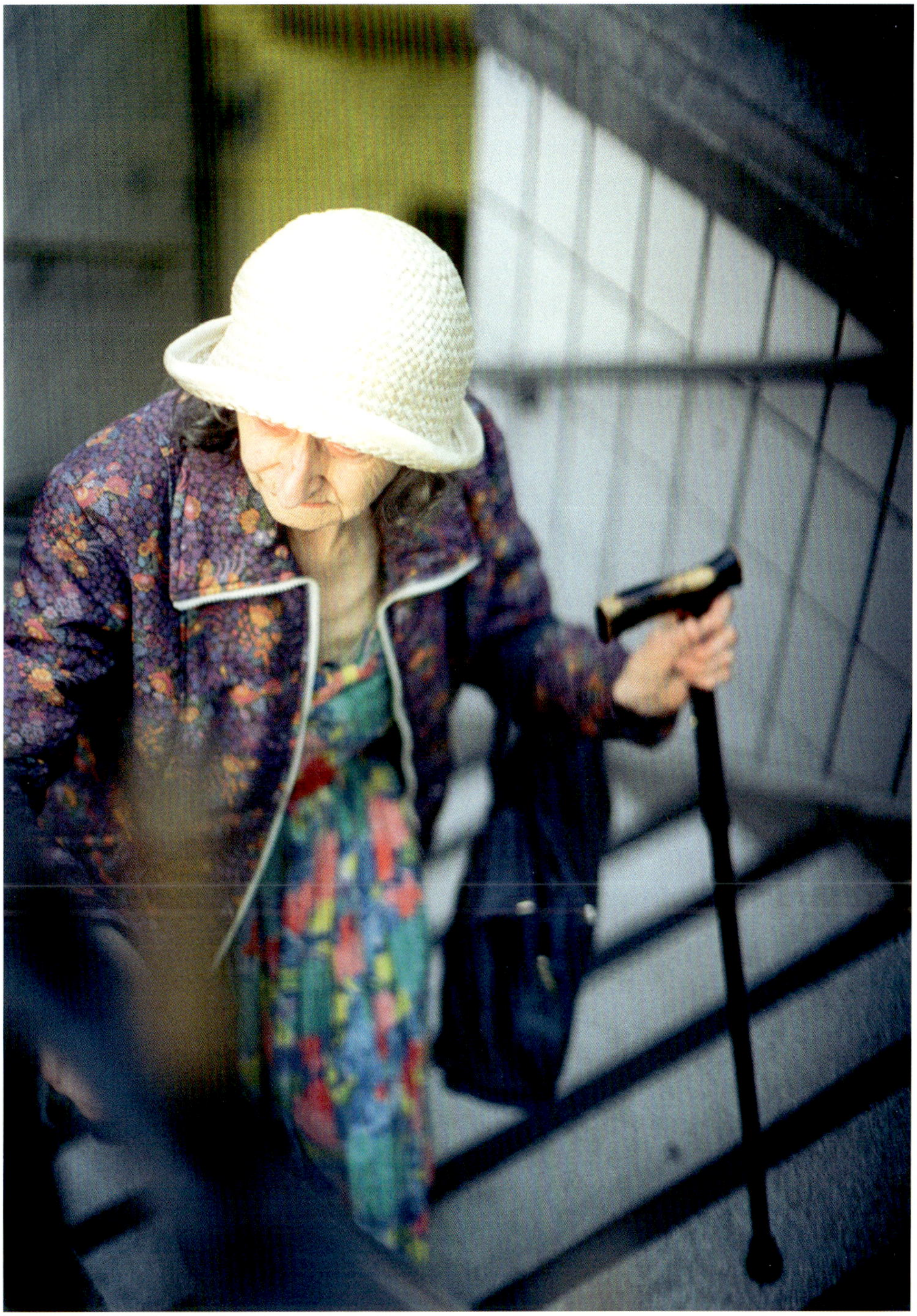

LEICESTER SQUARE
\
London – 2002

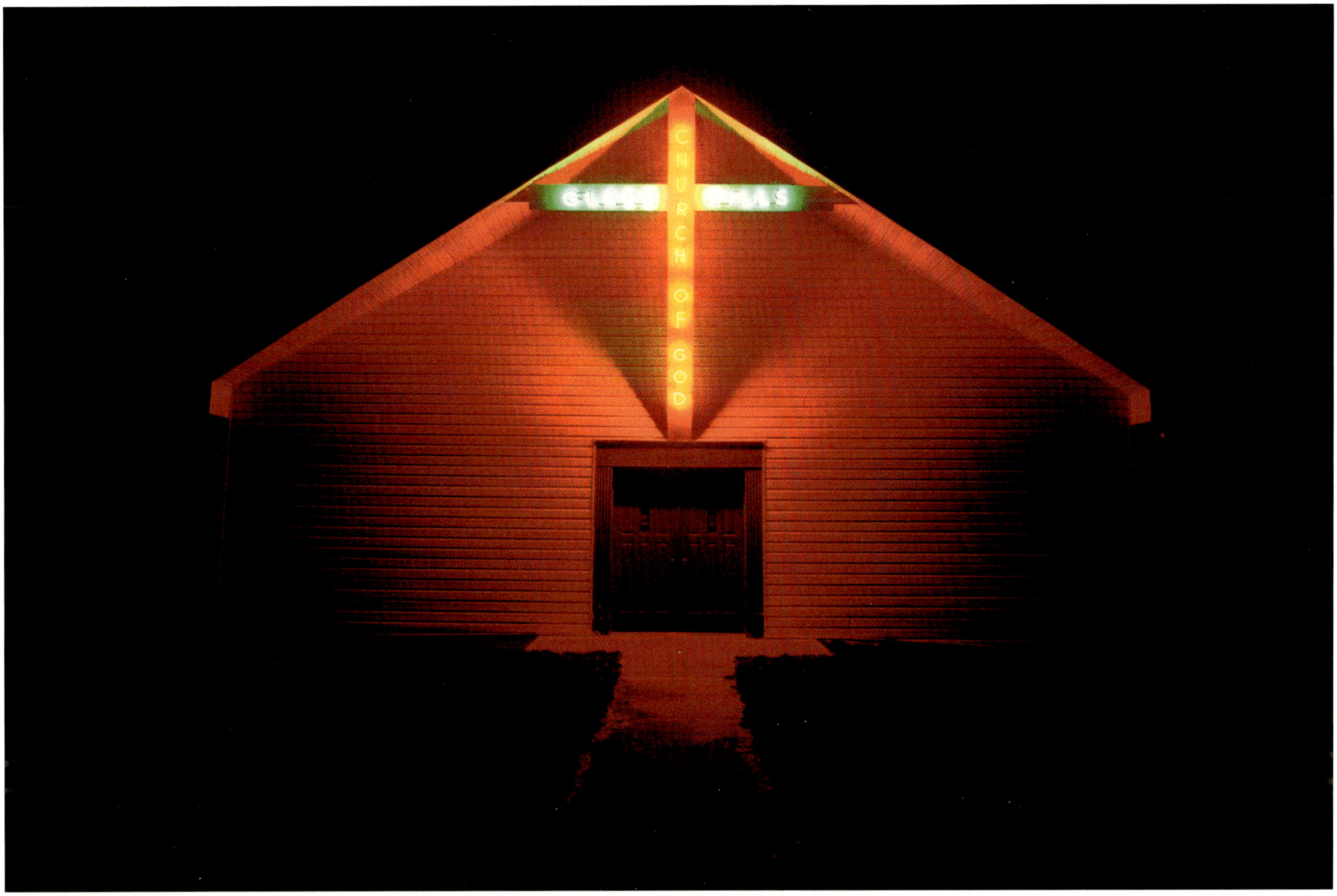

CHURCH OF GOD
\
Virginia – 2001

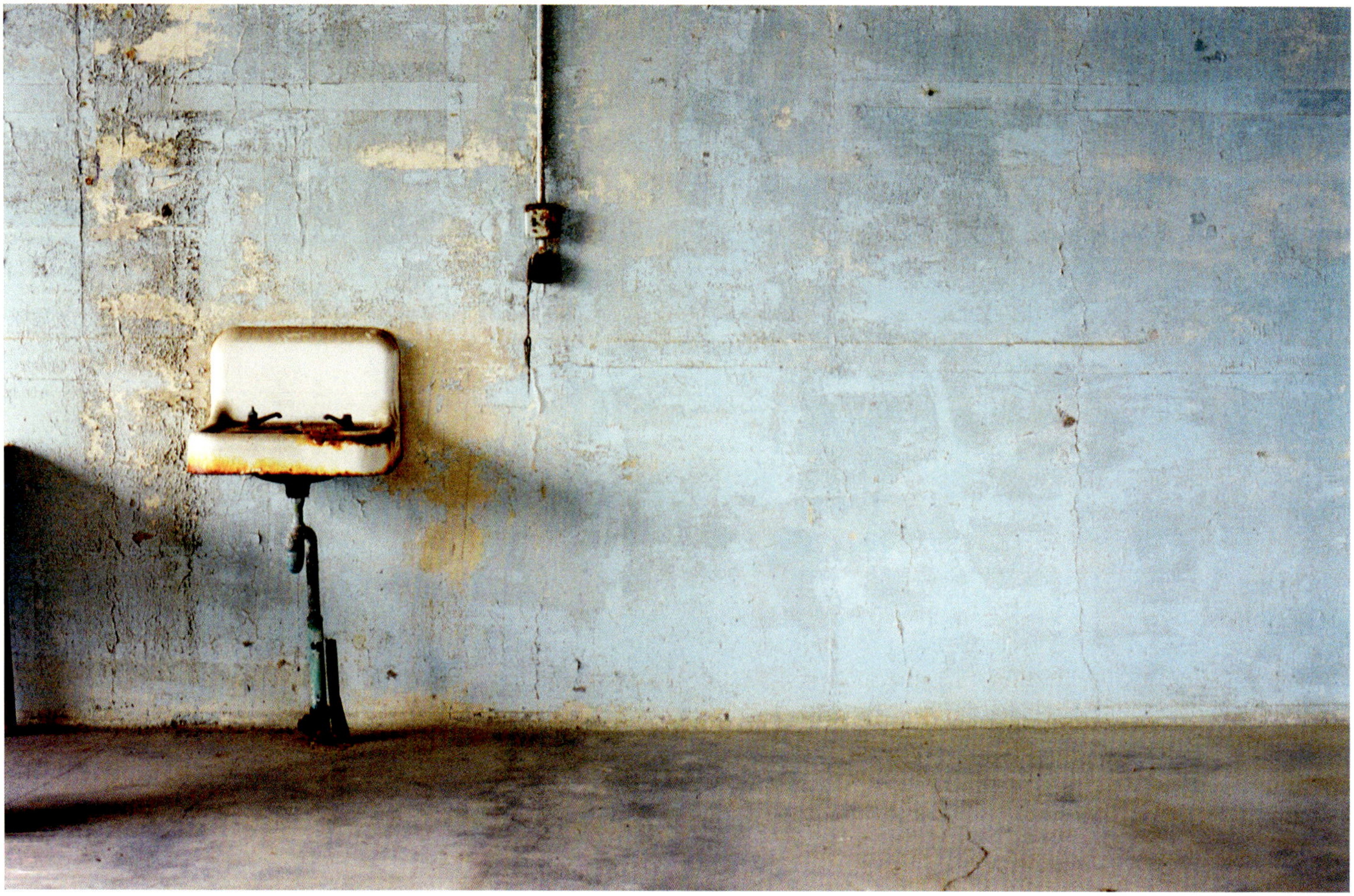

ALCATRAZ

\

San Francisco – 2005

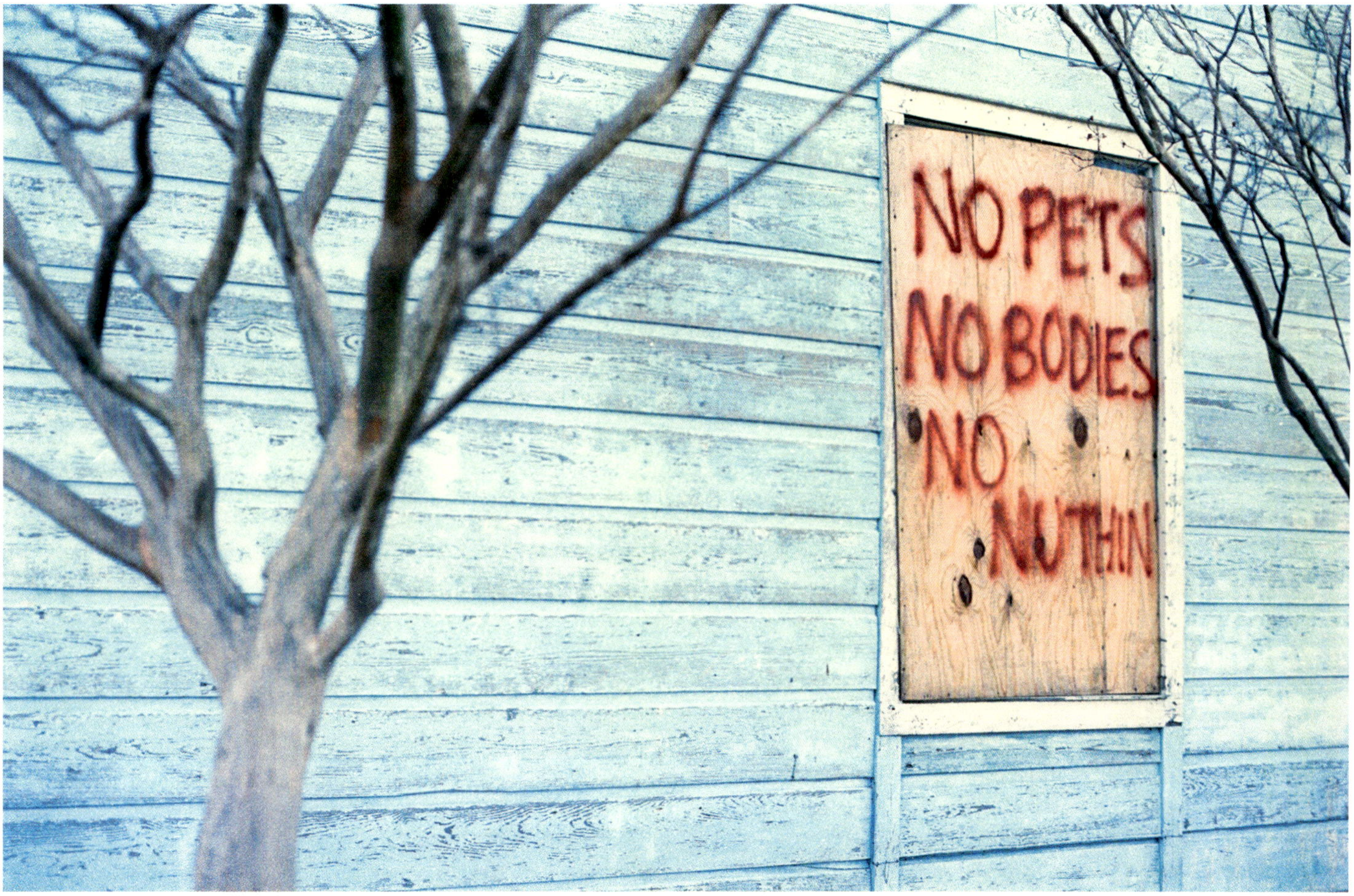

NO PETS

\

New Orleans – 2005

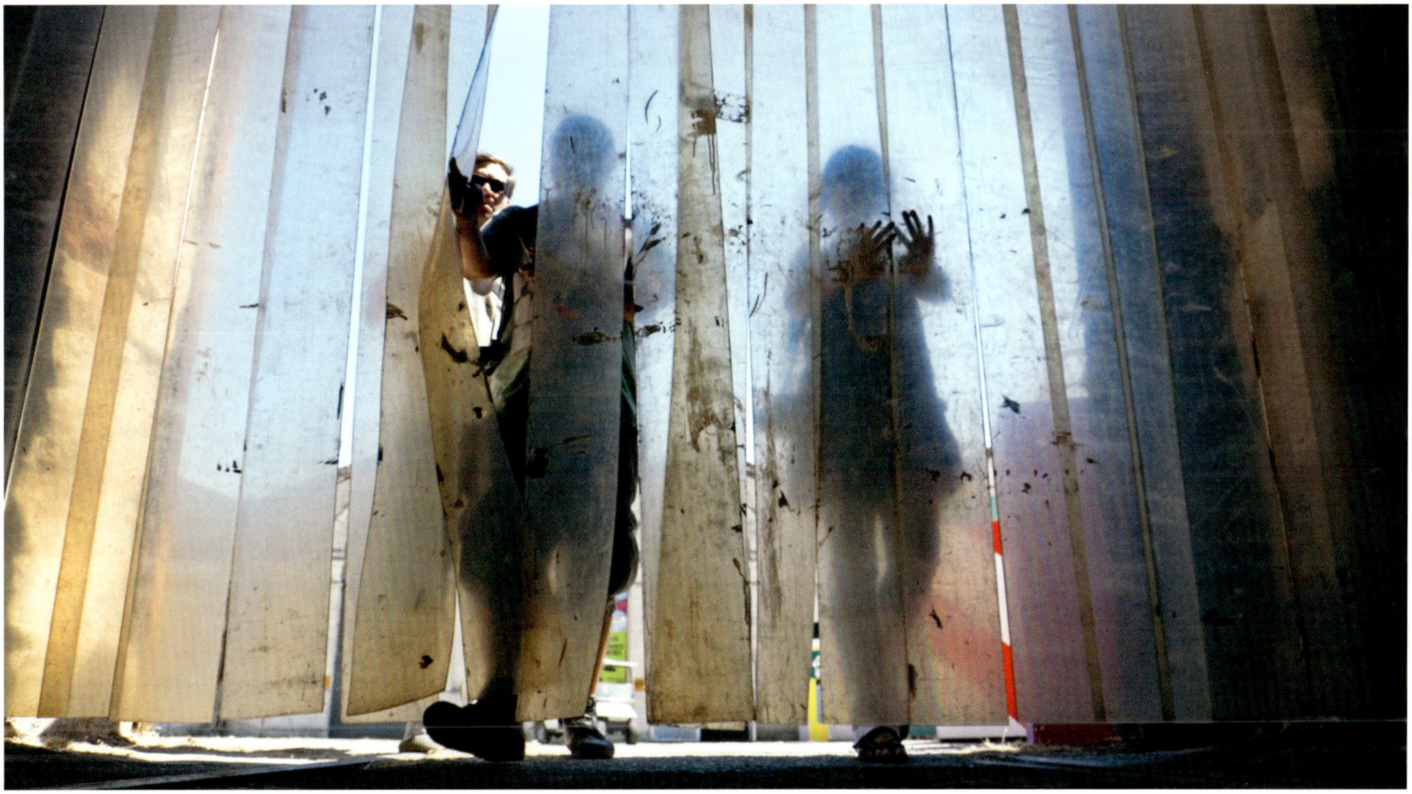

LES ATELIERS

\

Arles – 2010

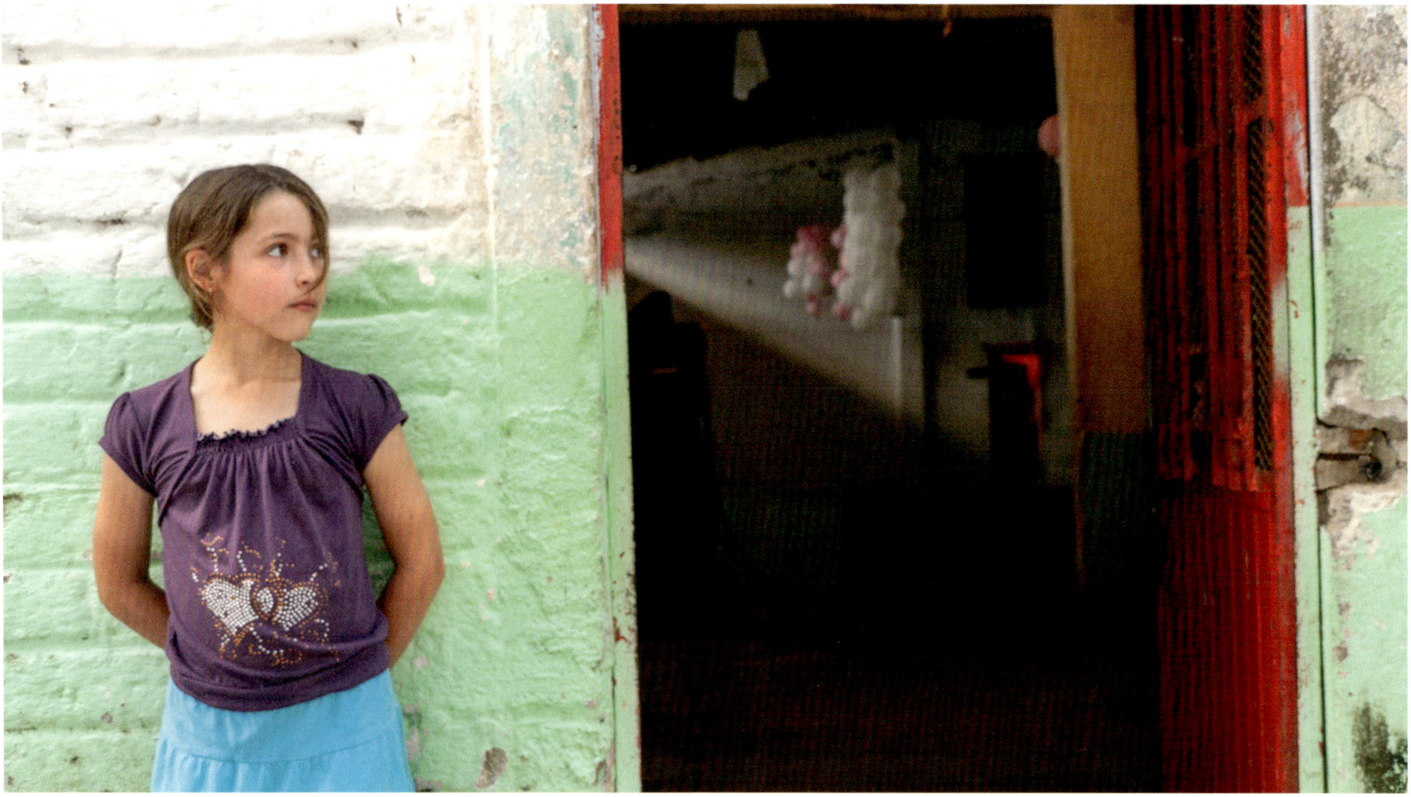

YELAPA
\
Mexico – 2011

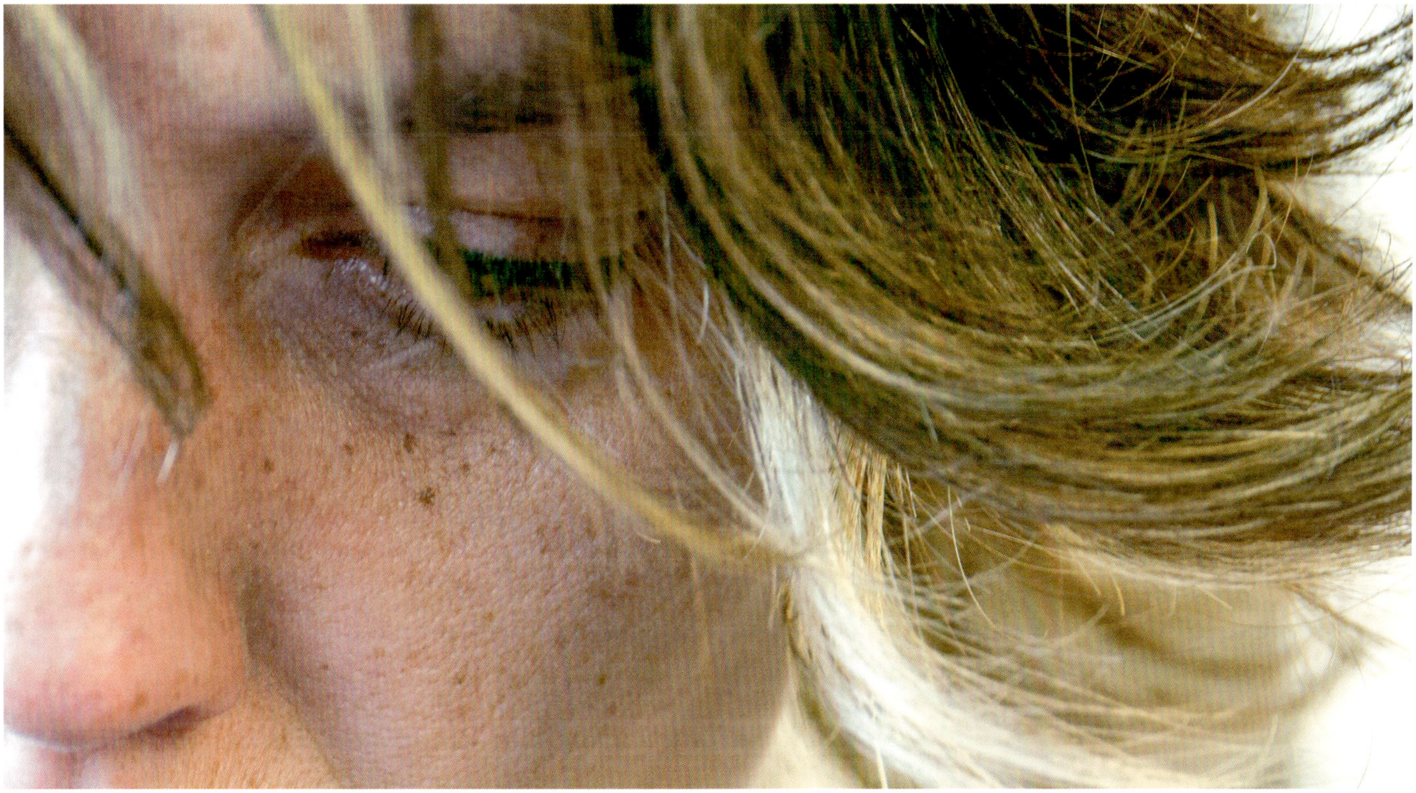

LOVE
\
Arles – 2010

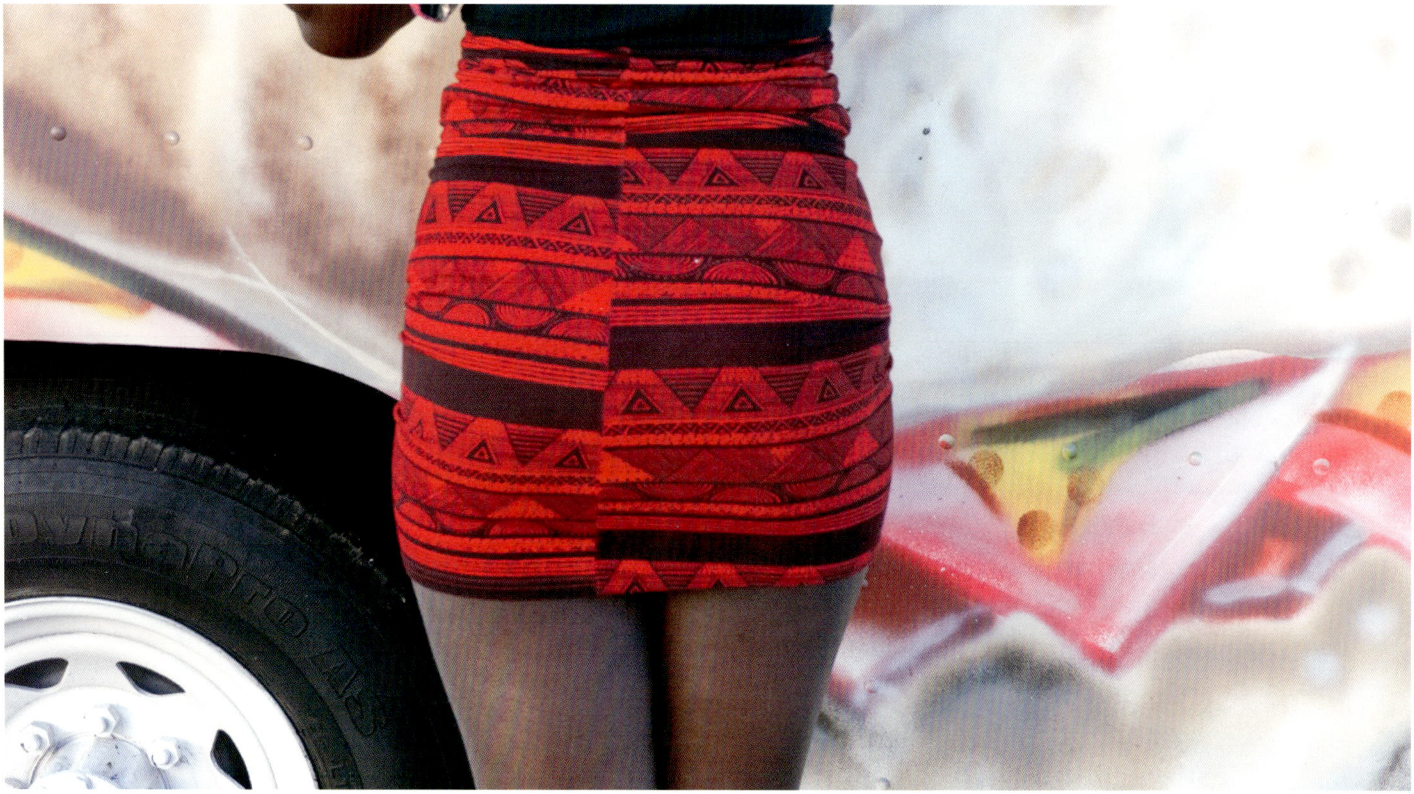

SAINT JOSEPH'S DAY

\

New Orleans – 2011

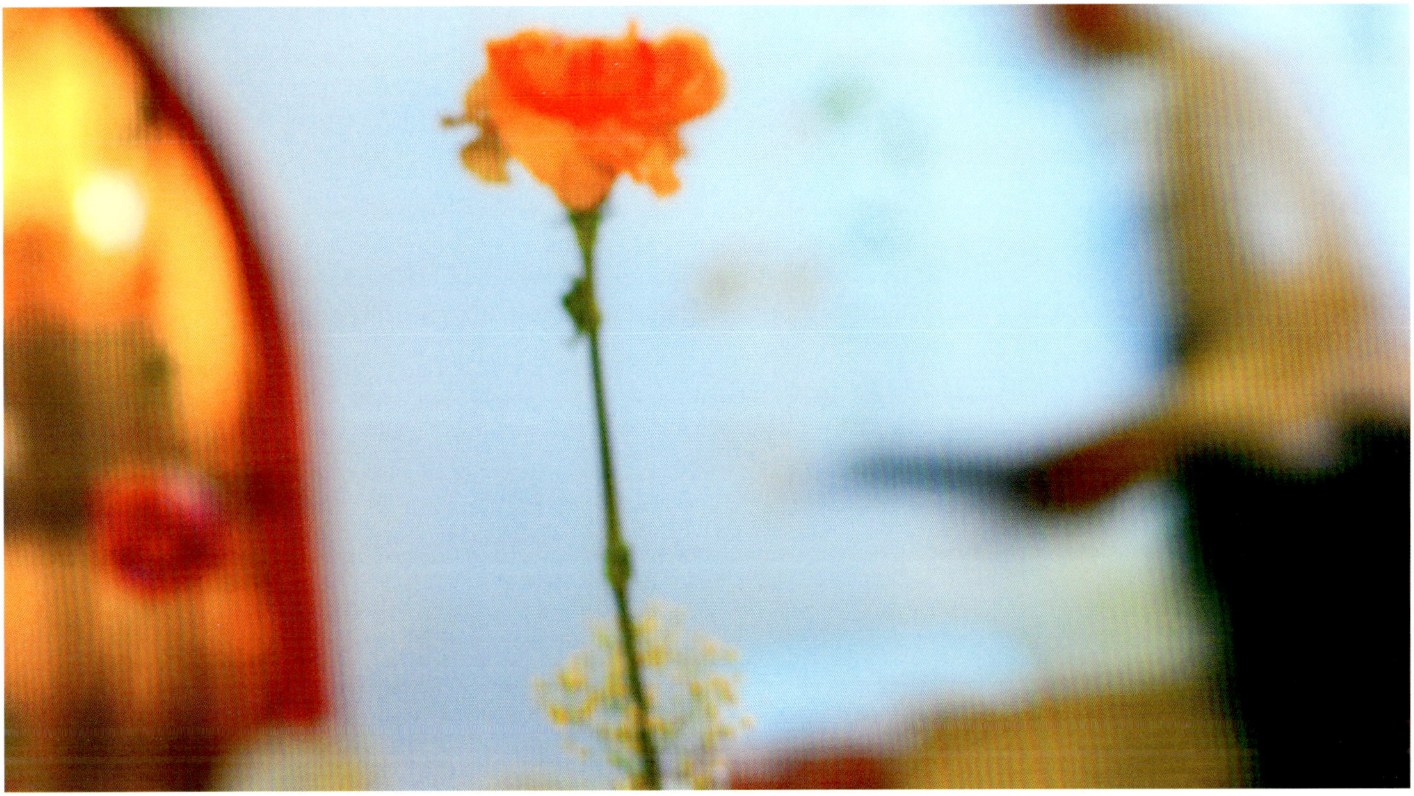

SAN JUAN
\
Puerto Rico – 2011

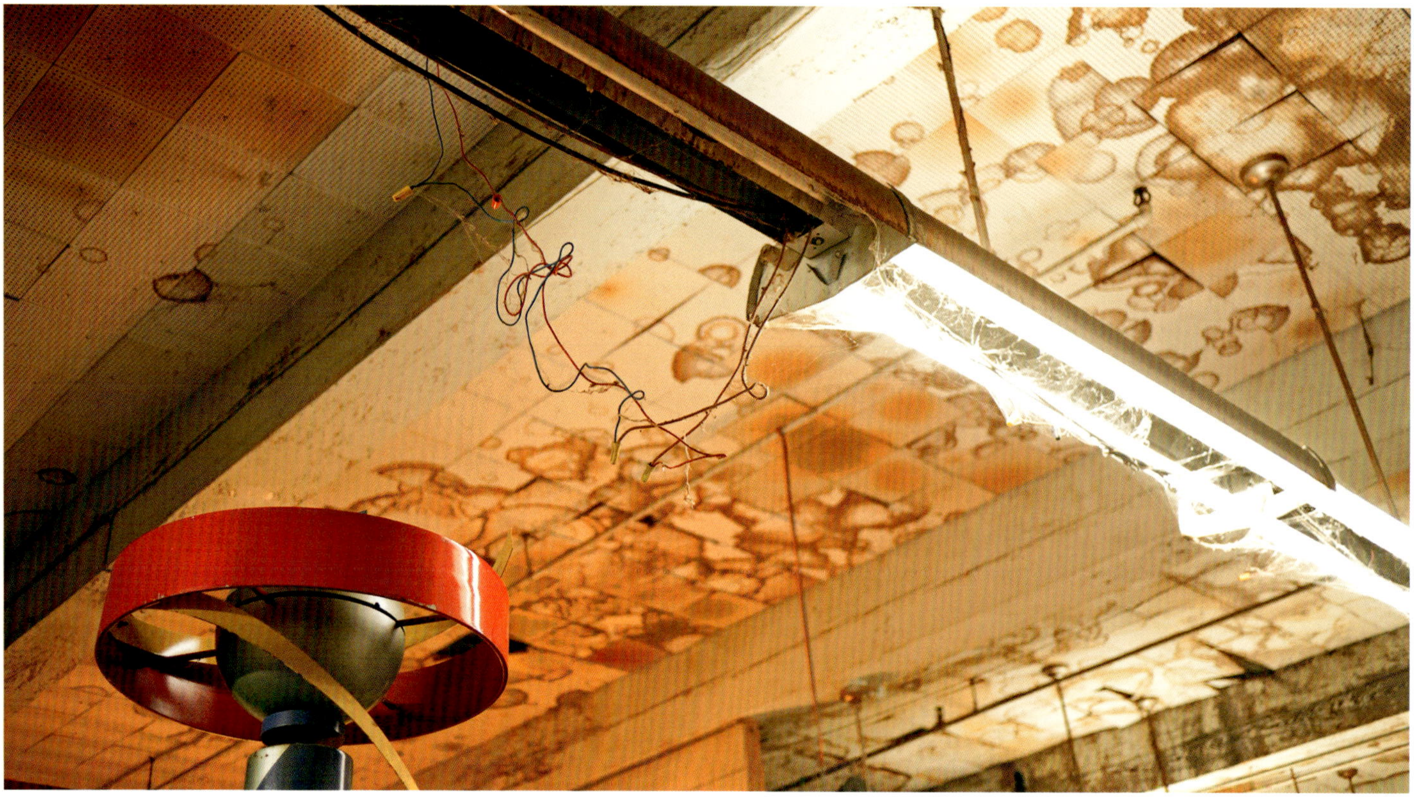

ABANDONED ARC
\
New Orleans – 2012

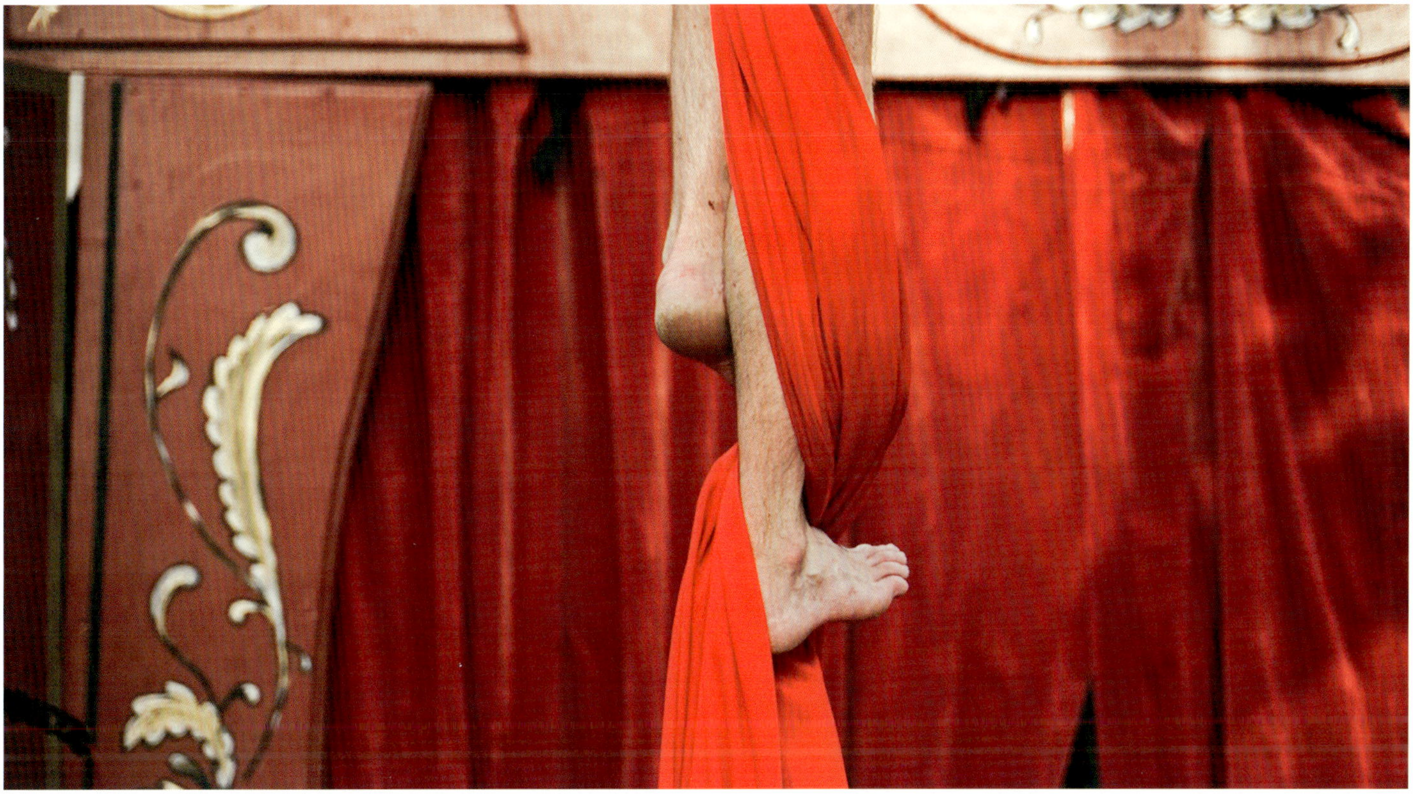

CIRQUE
\
Avignon – 2010

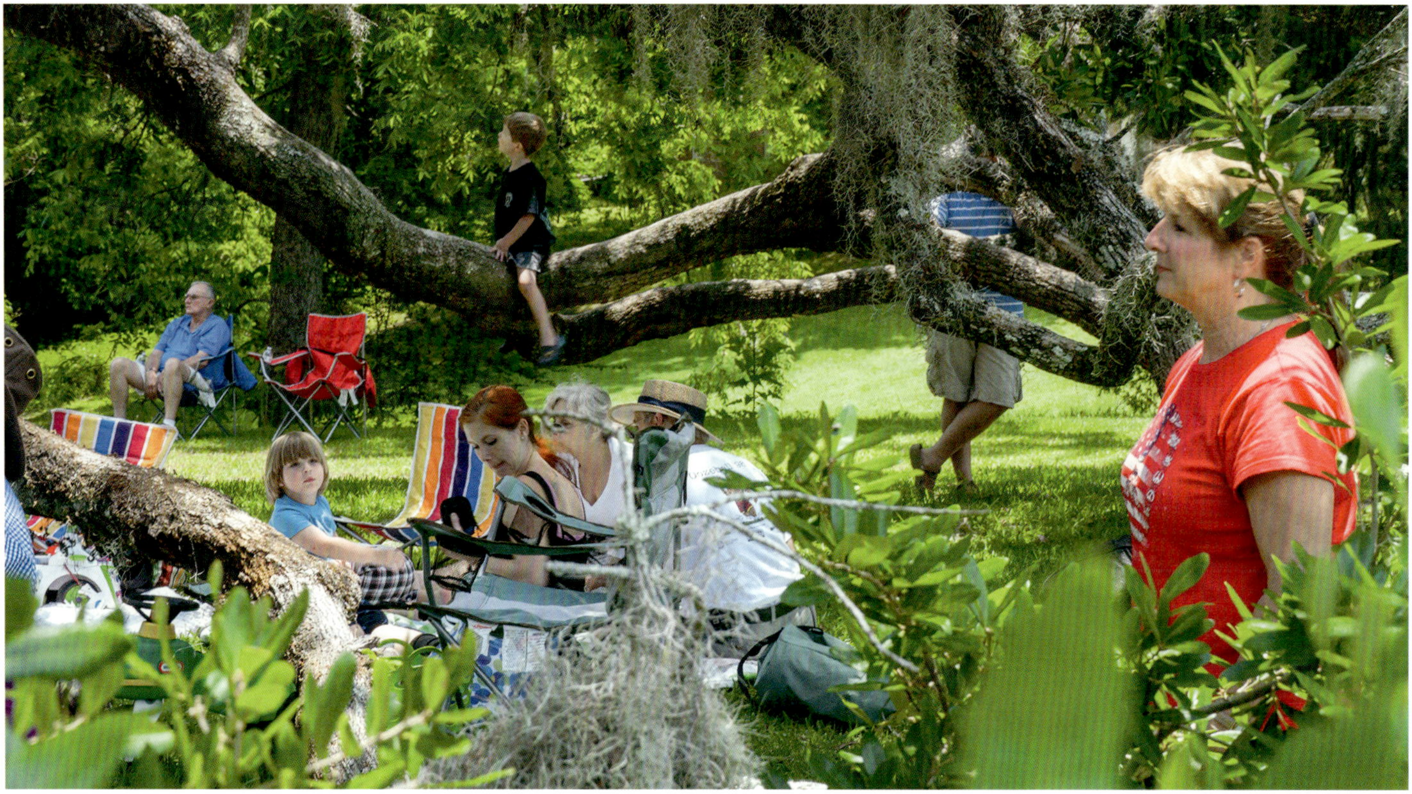

BIG YAM FEST

\

Mississippi – 2011

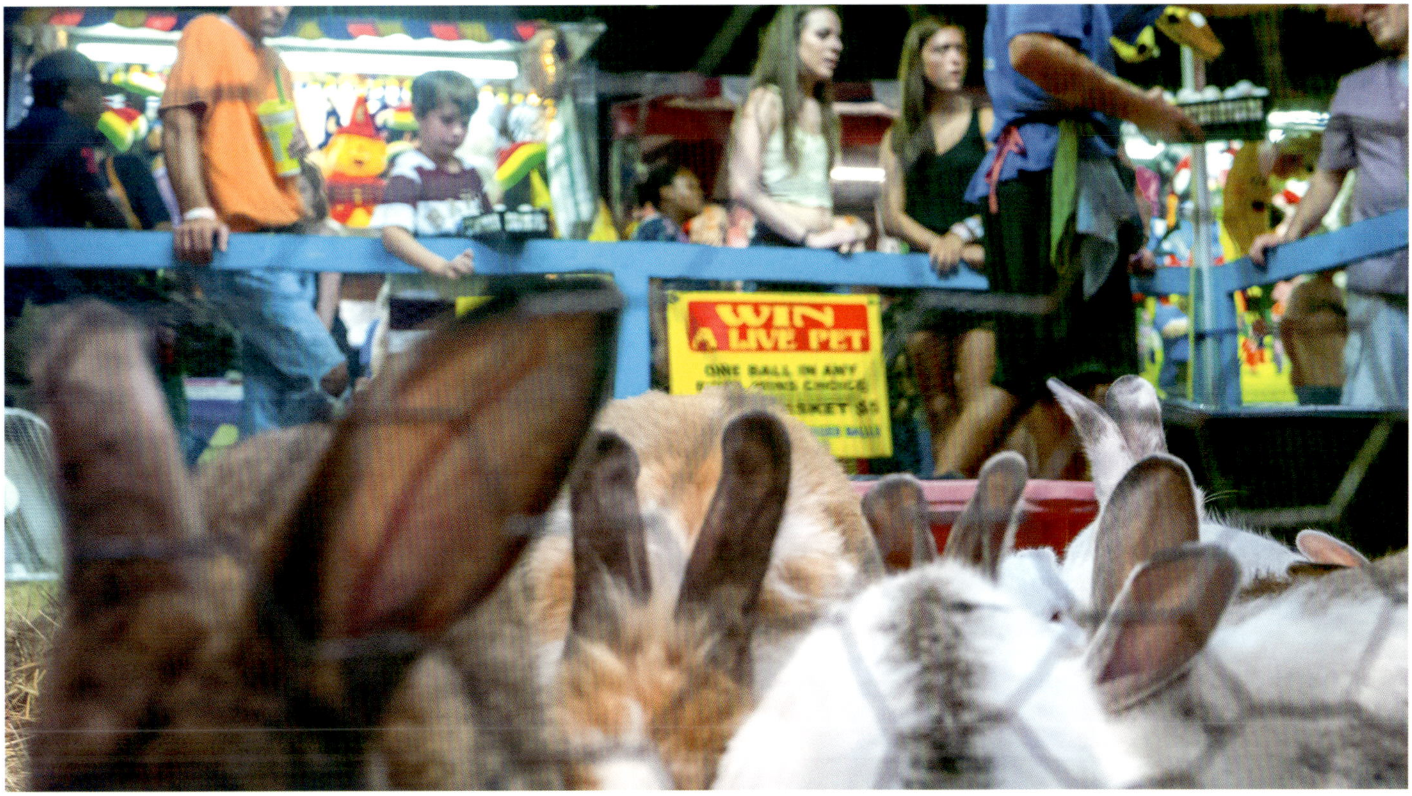

NESHOBA COUNTY FAIR
\
Mississippi – 2011

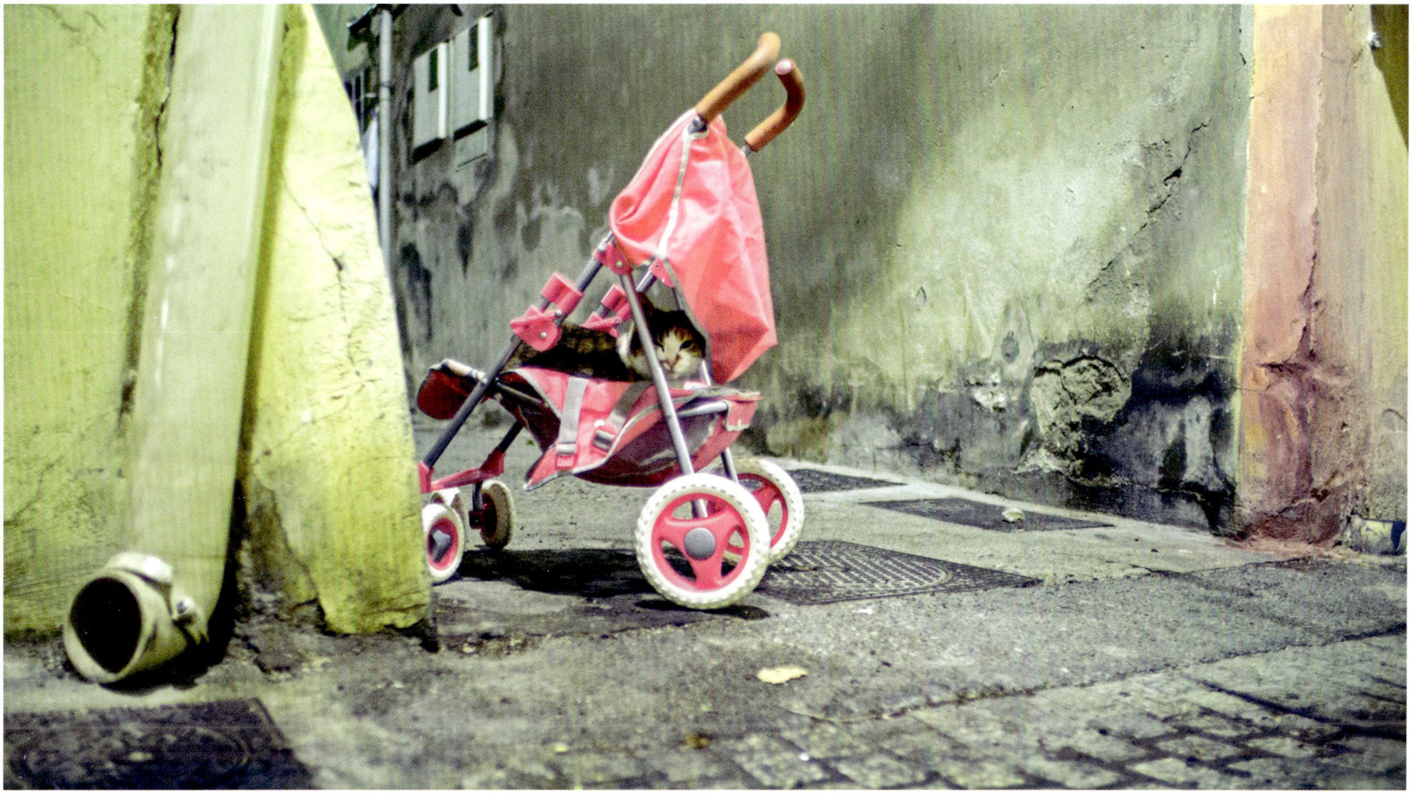

KITTY IN BABY BUGGY

\

Arles – 2013

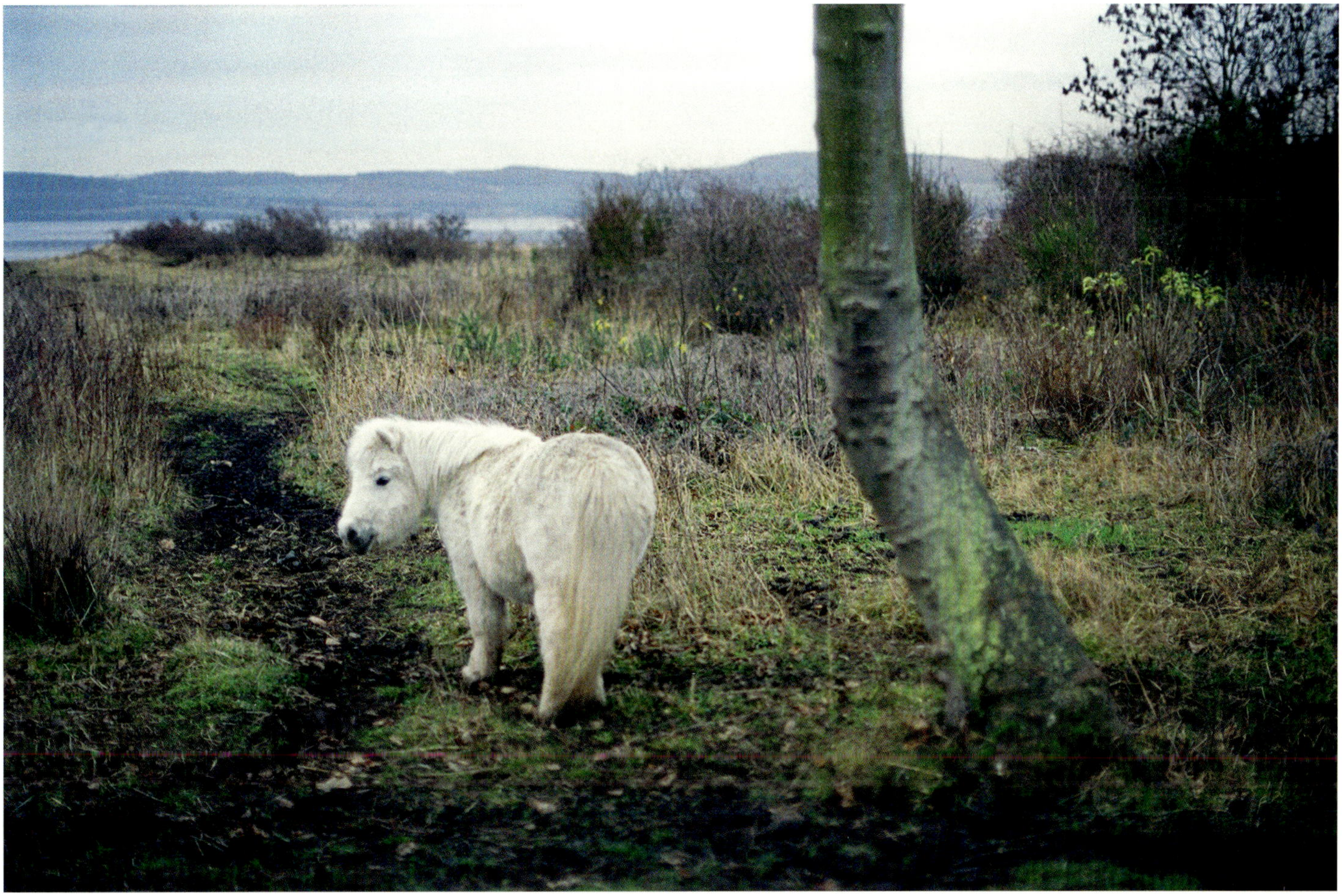

PONY
\
Scotland – 2003

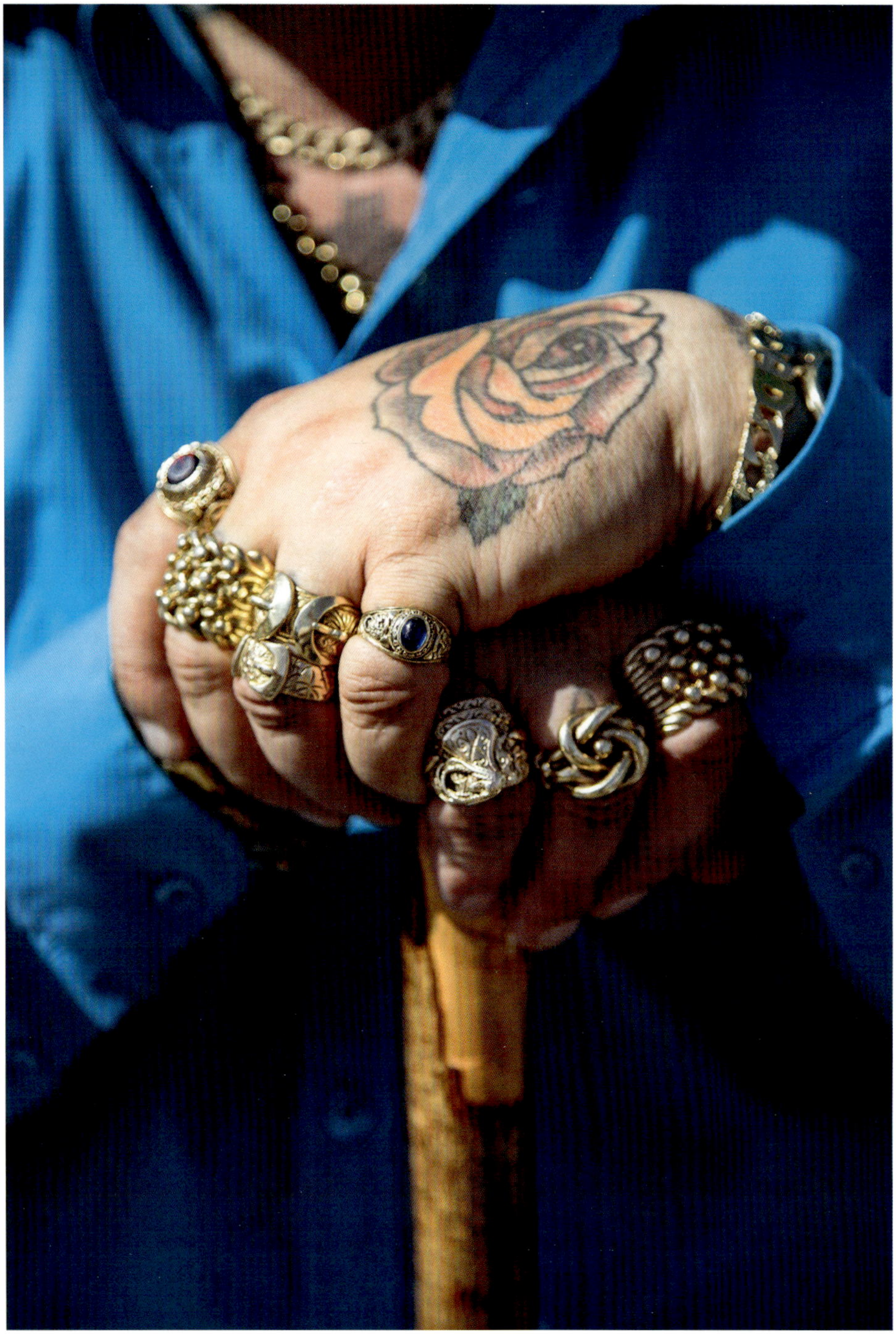

WILLIAM OF CORK

\

Ireland – 2014

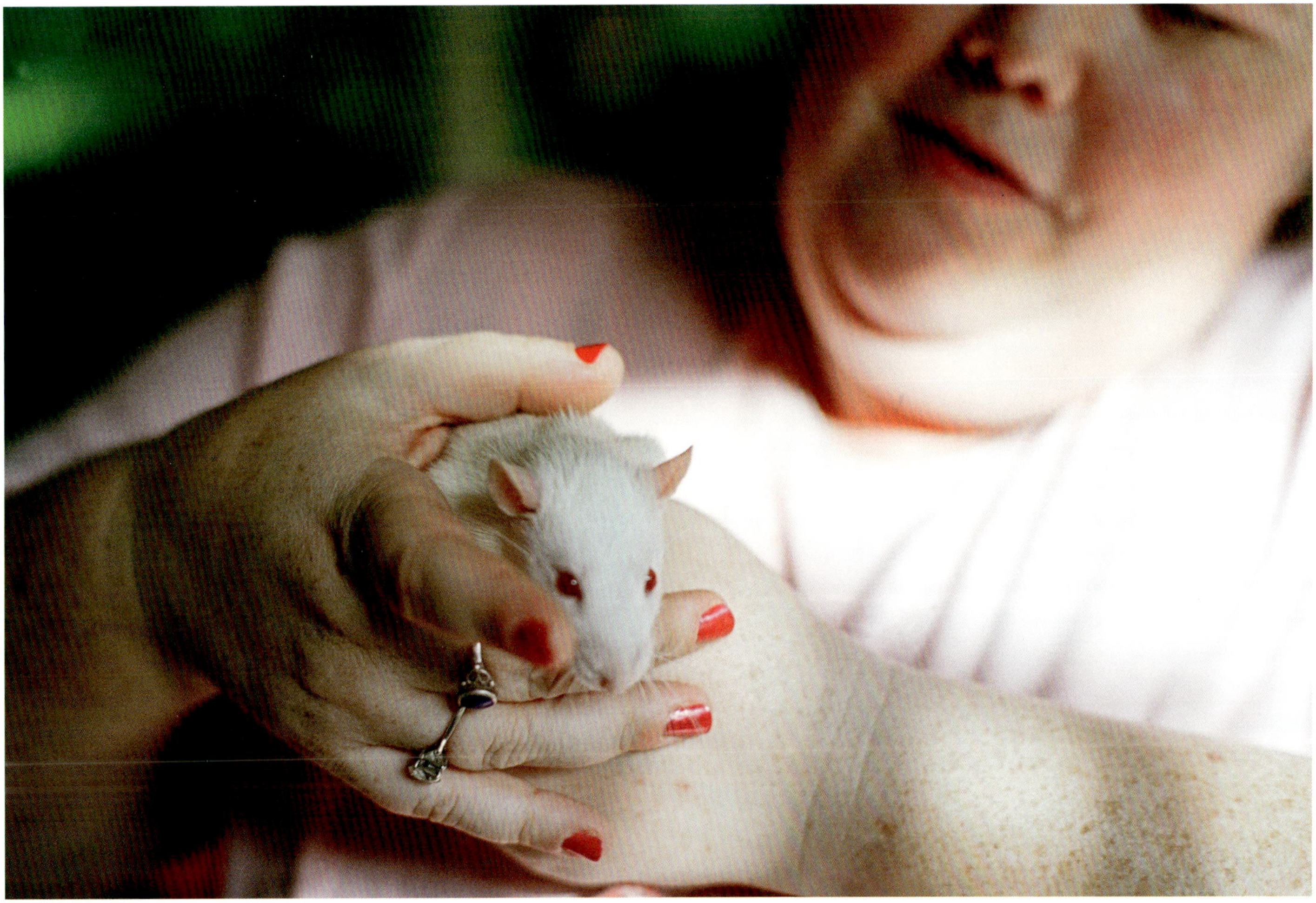

DEBBIE & SUCKATOOTH
\
Memphis – 2008

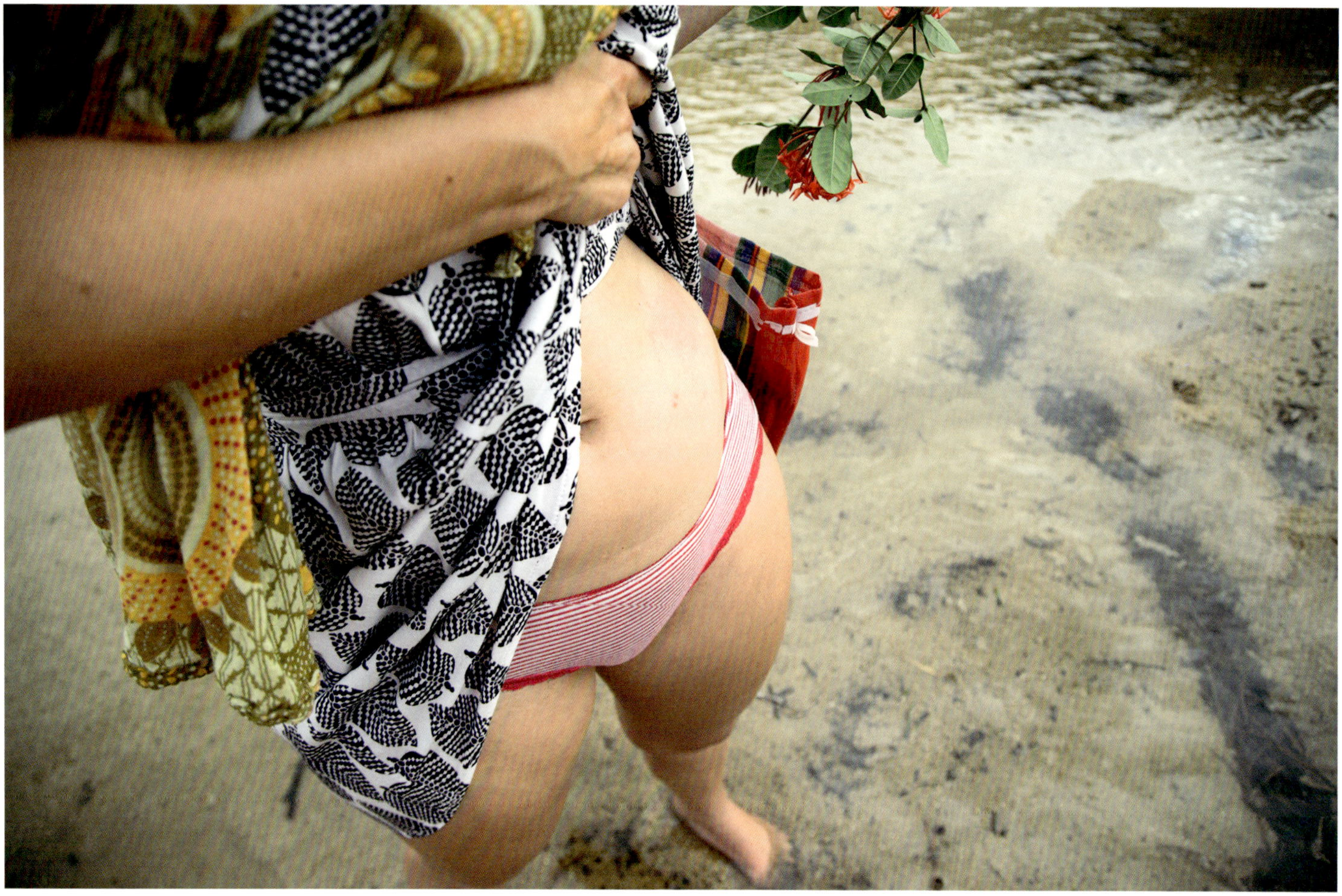

VALENTINE
\
Yelapa – 2015

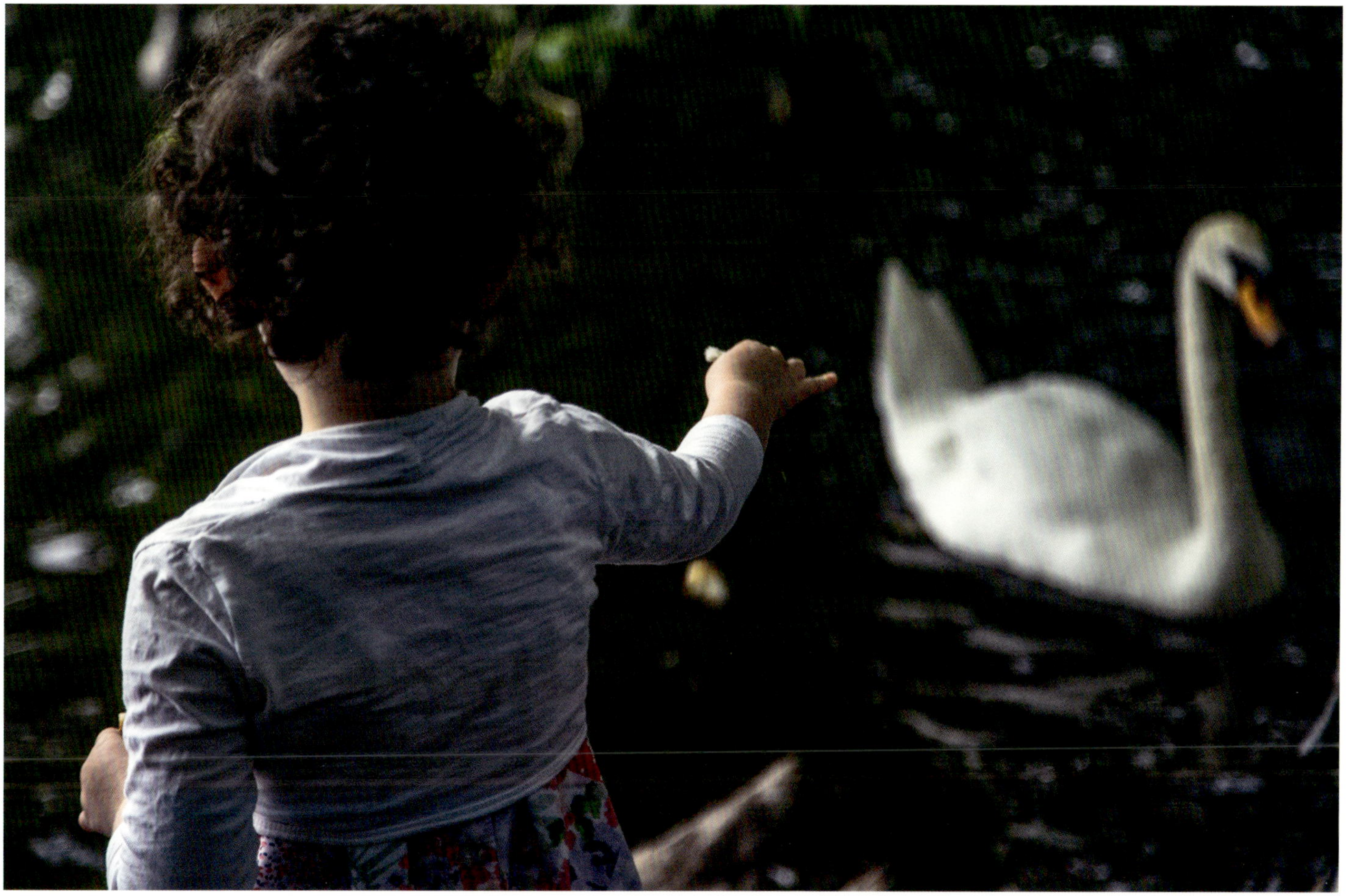

SAINT STEPHEN'S GREEN
\
Dublin – 2014

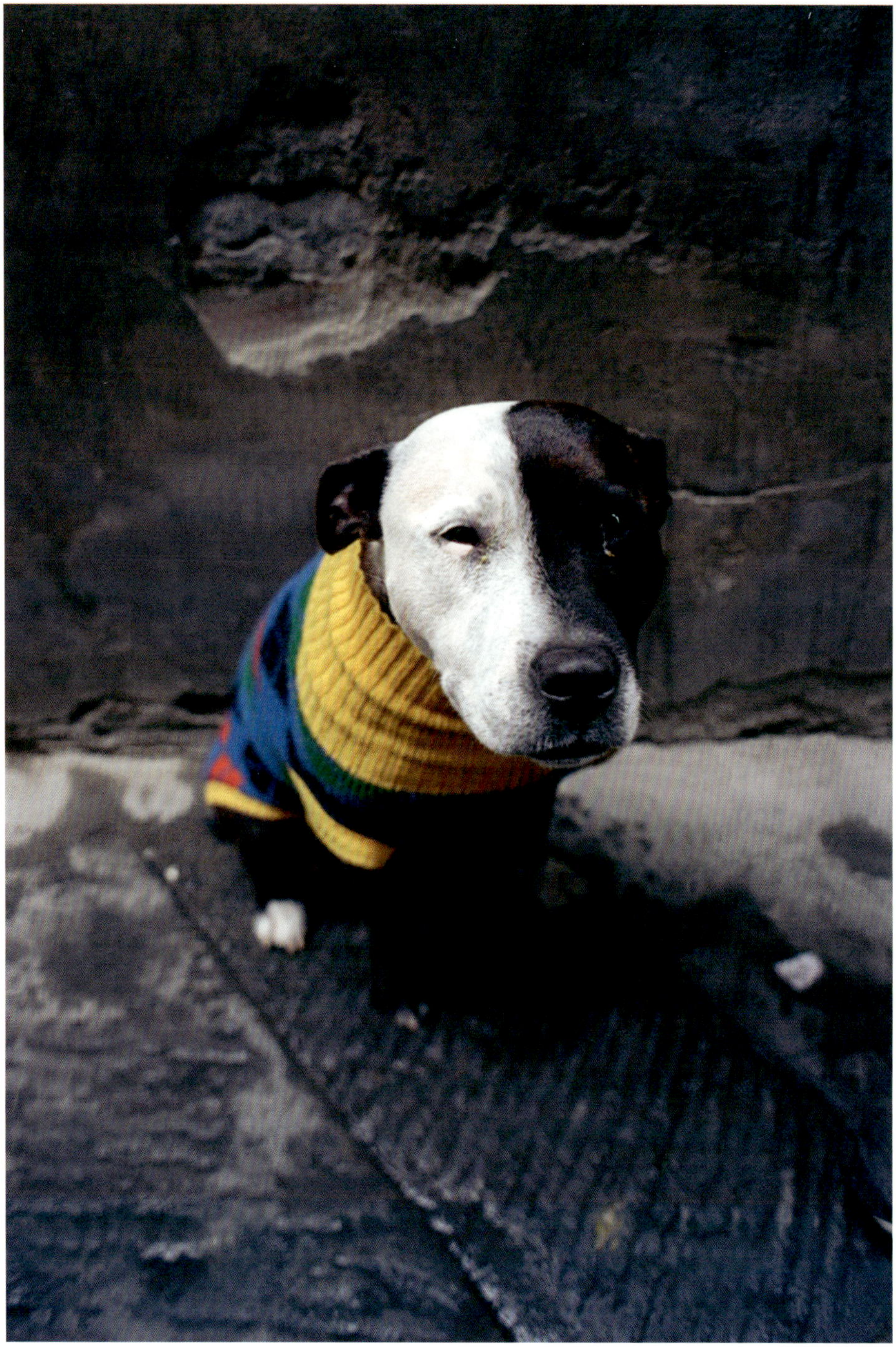

SCOTTISH DOG IN SIENA
\
Italy – 1997

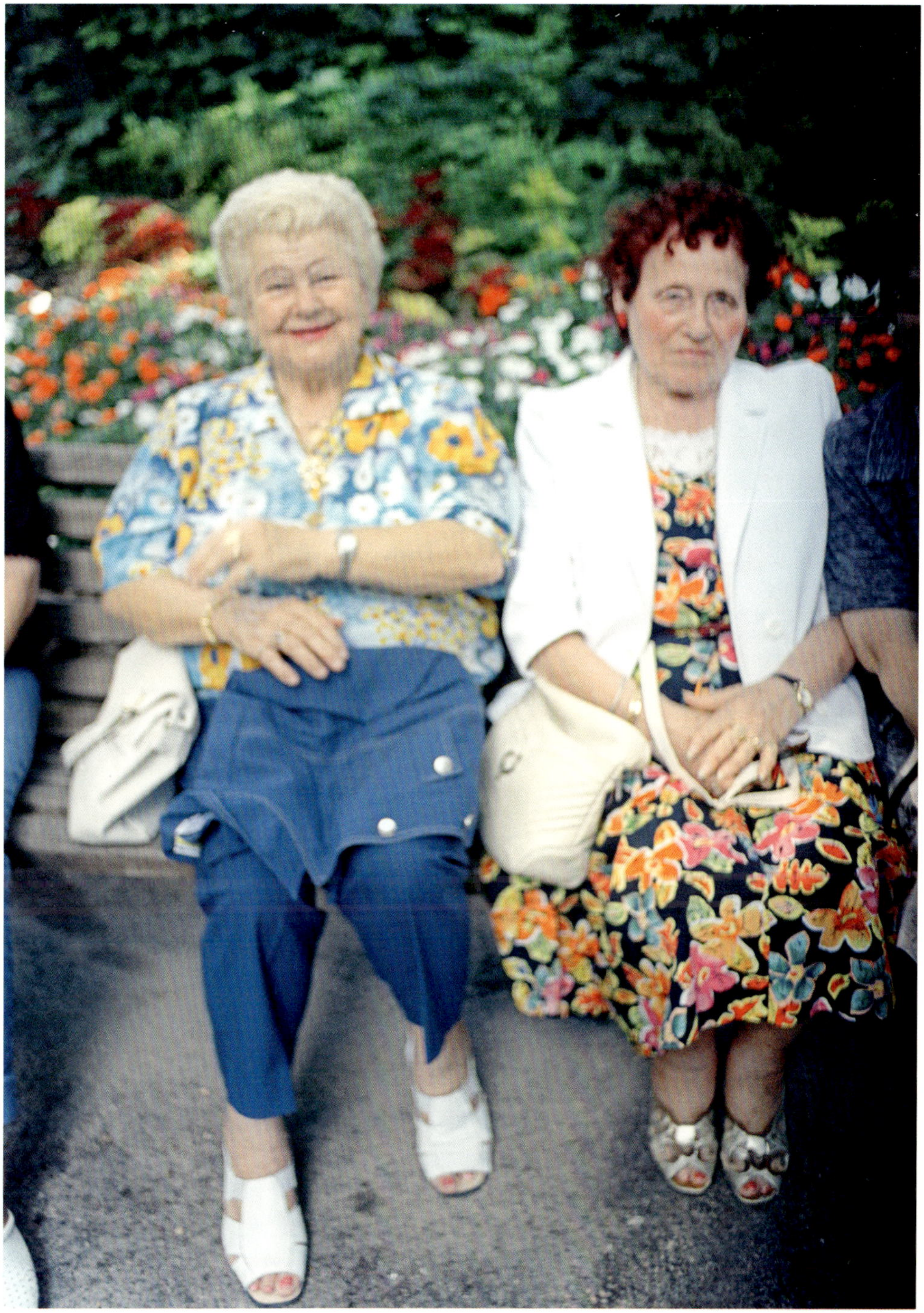

LES JARDINS
\
Arles – 2002

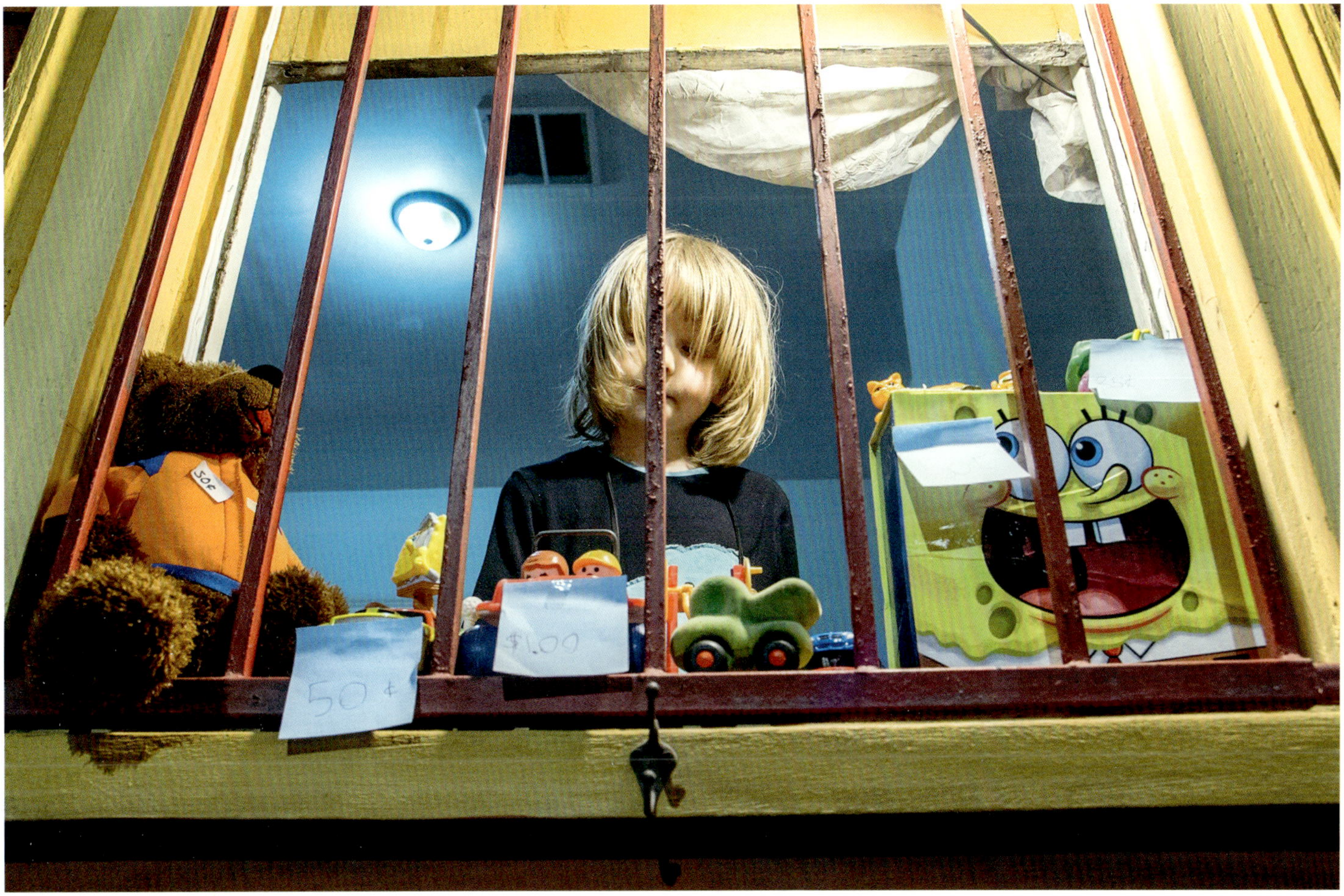

ART SALE

\

New Orleans – 2015

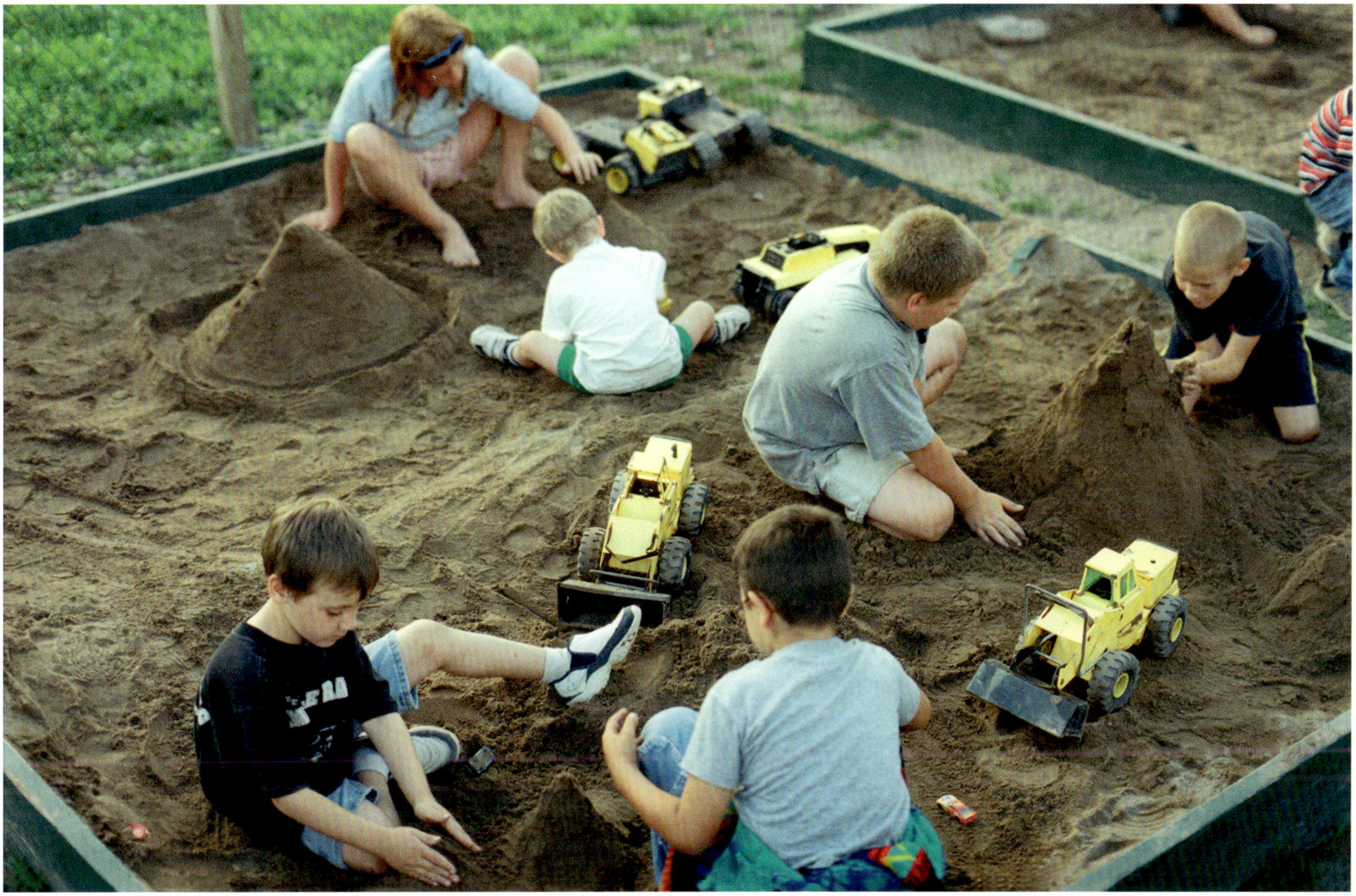

SANDBOX

\

Hudson Valley, NY – 2002

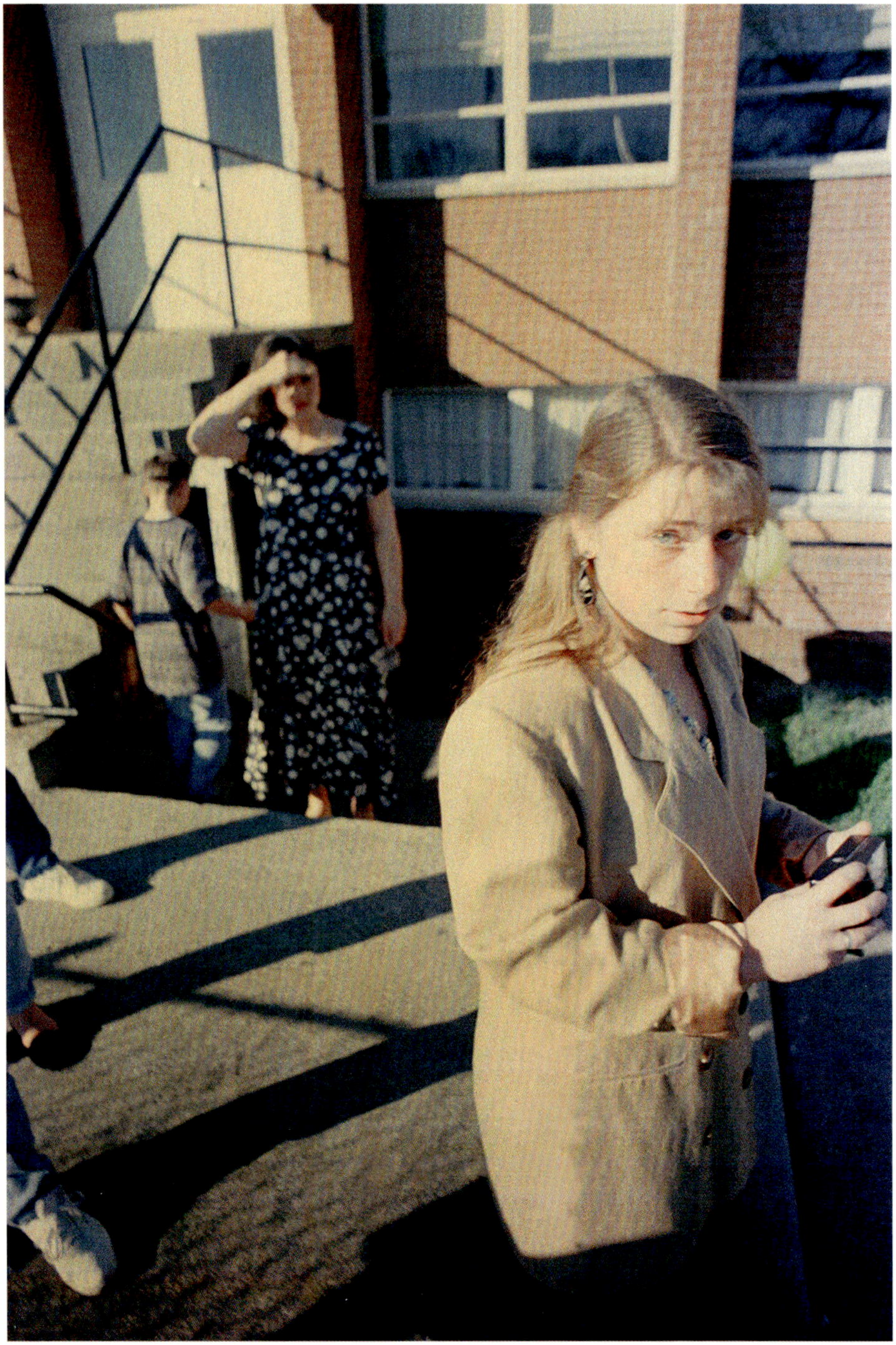

3 COUSINS WITH THE FEET AND SHADOWS OF THREE MORE COUSINS

\

North Carolina – 1994

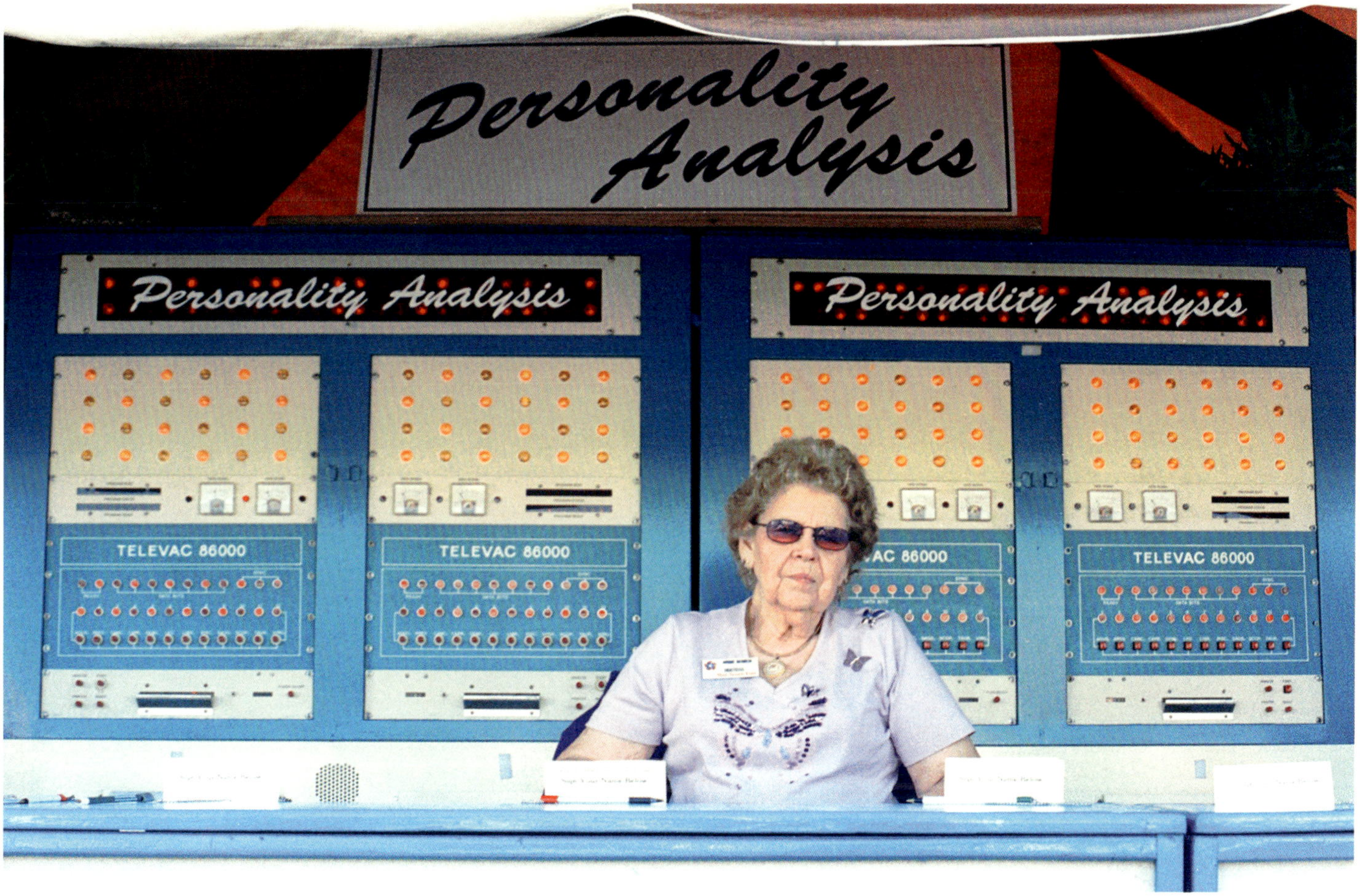

PERSONALITY ANALYSIS BOOTH
\
Memphis – 2002

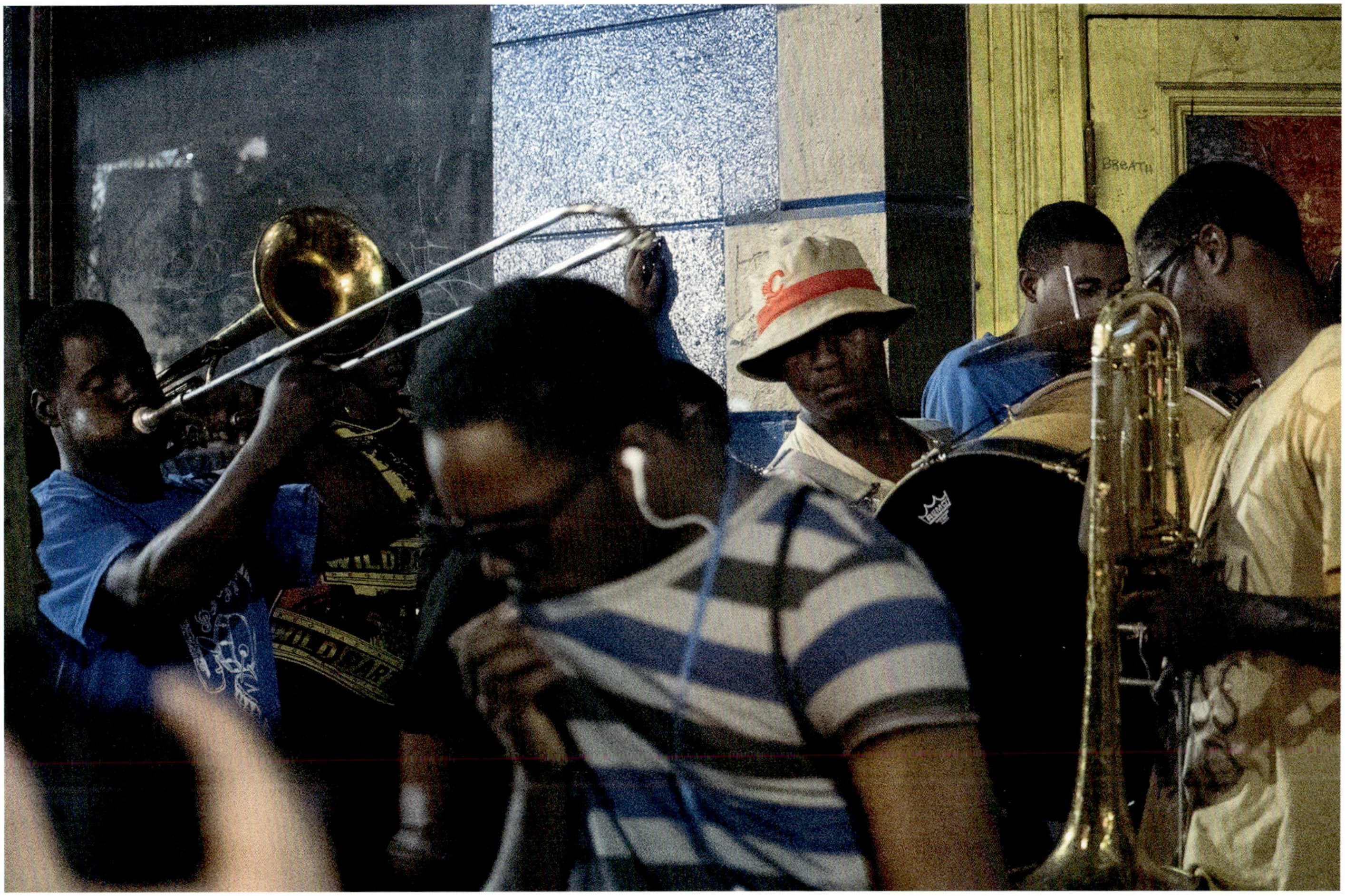

FRENCHMEN STREET

\

New Orleans – 2014

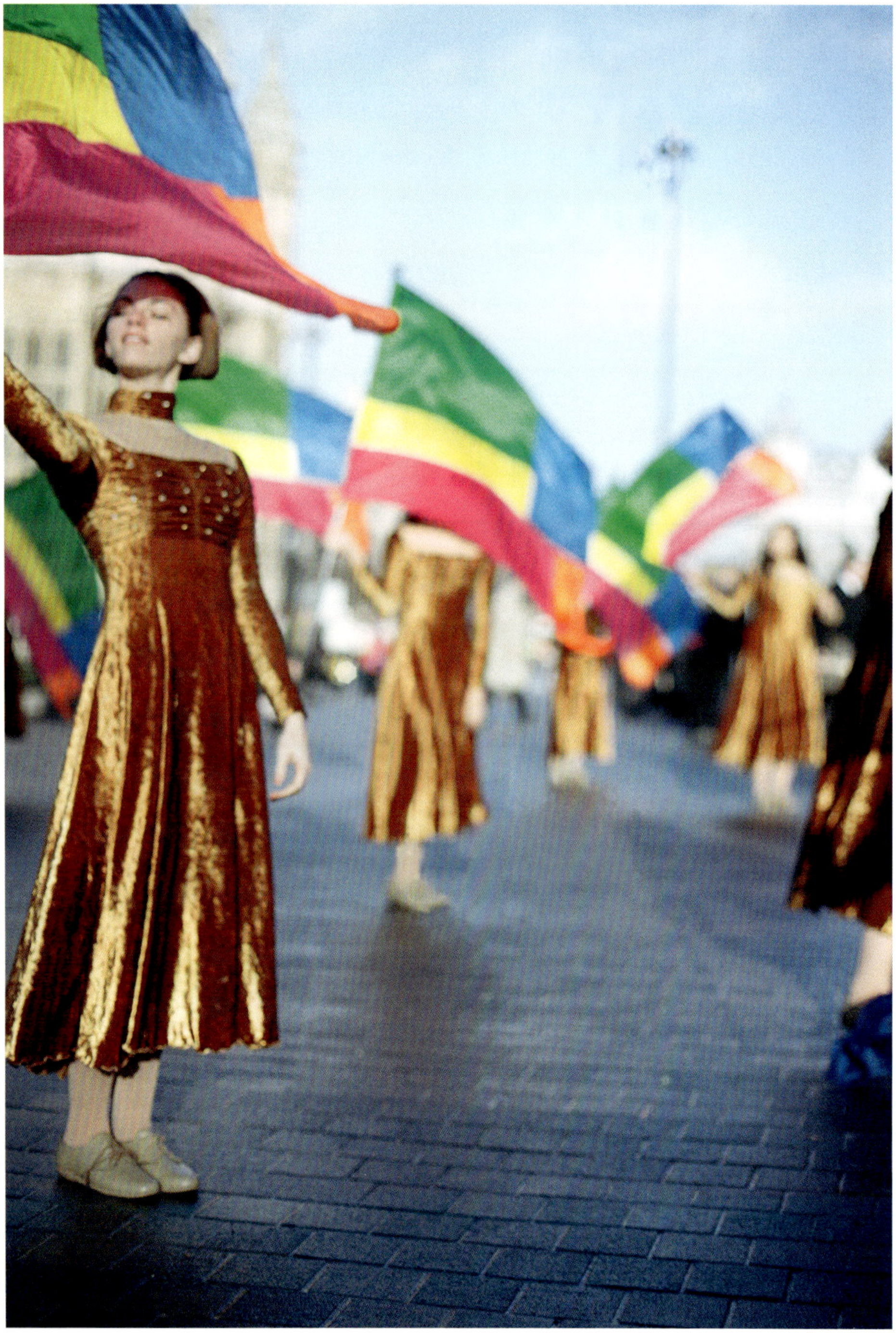

FLAG GIRLS
\
London – 1999

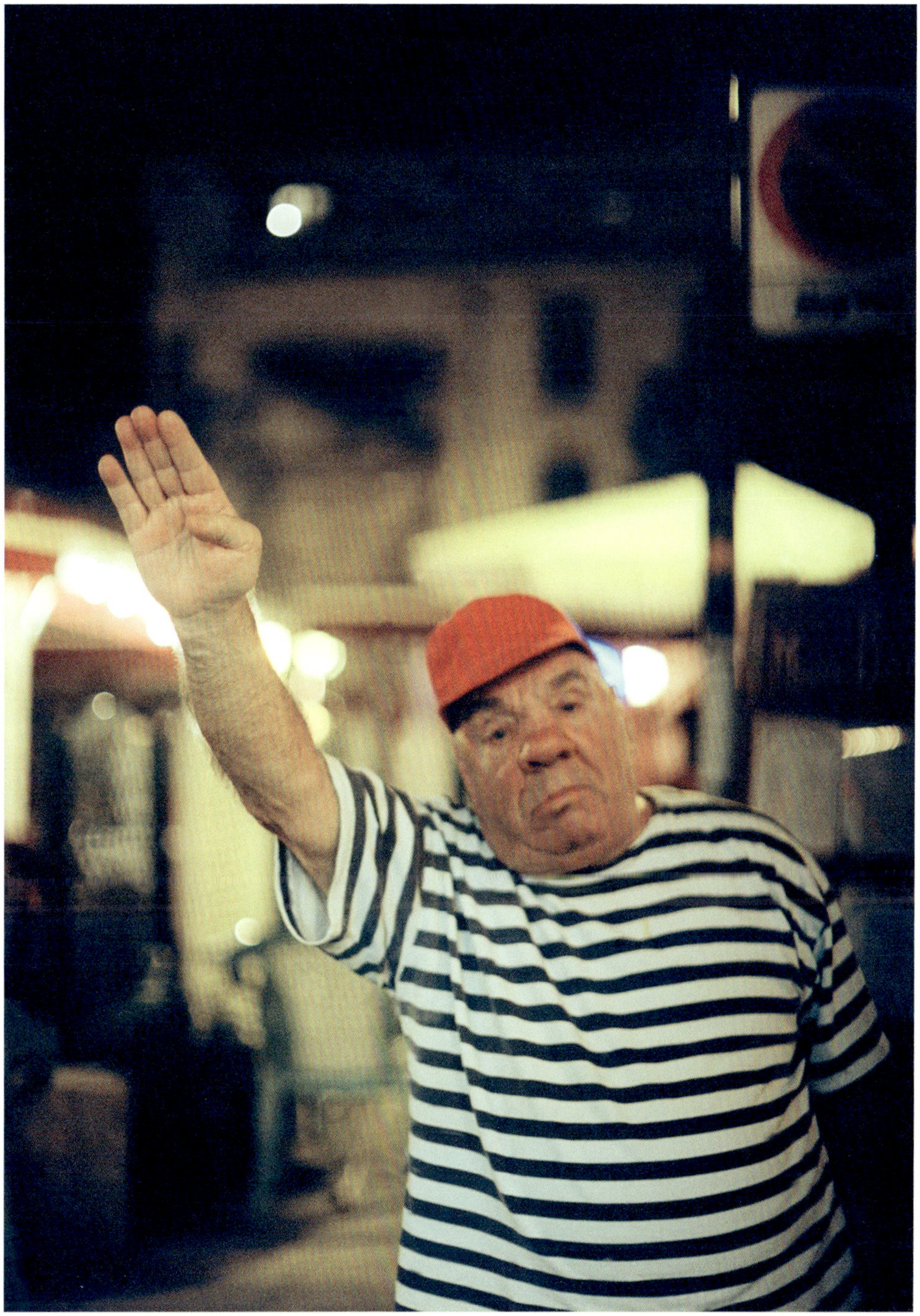

PLACE DU FORUM
\
Arles – 2002

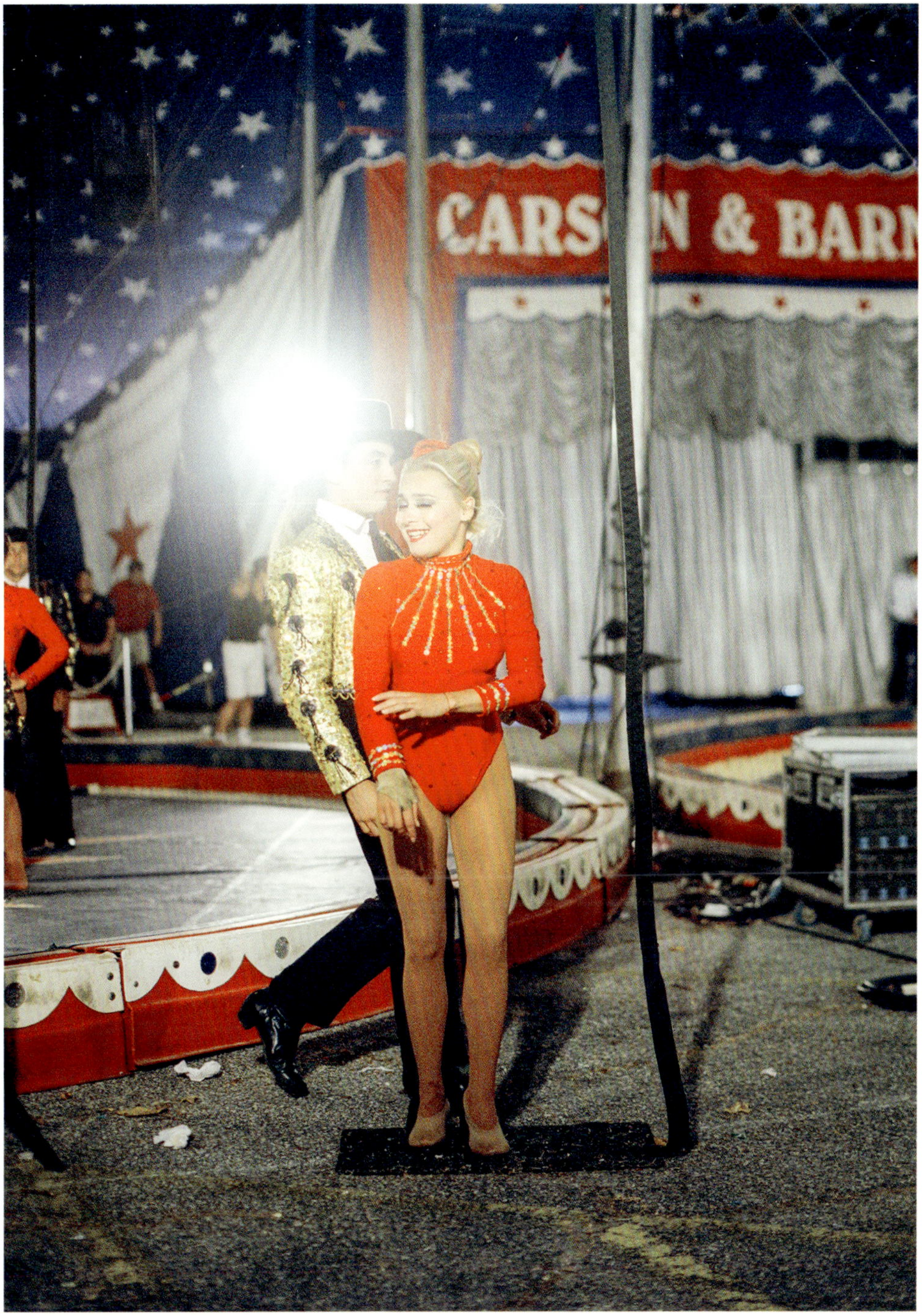

BIG TOP CIRCUS
\
Memphis – 2002

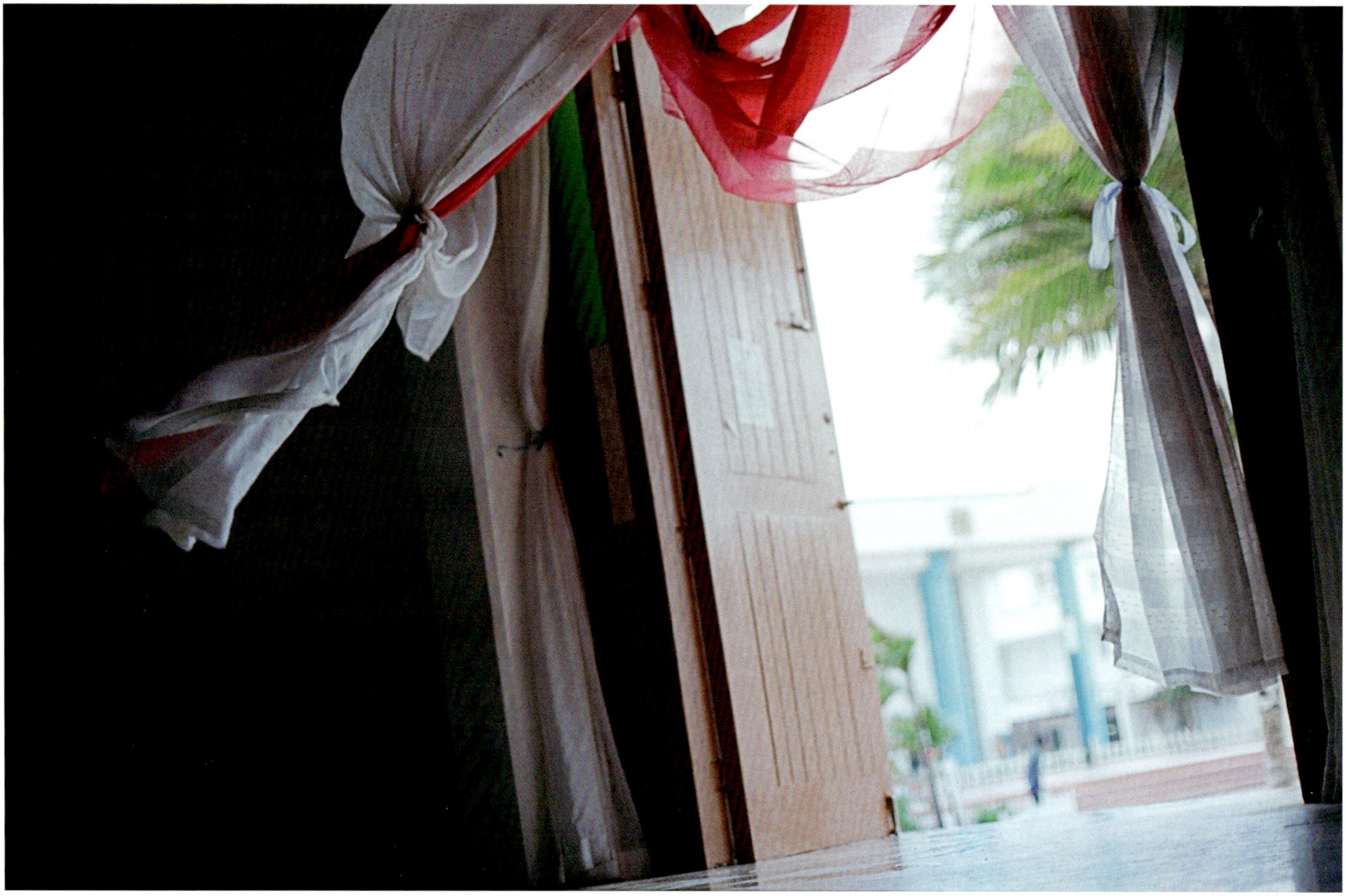

ISLA MUJERES

\

Mexico – 2010

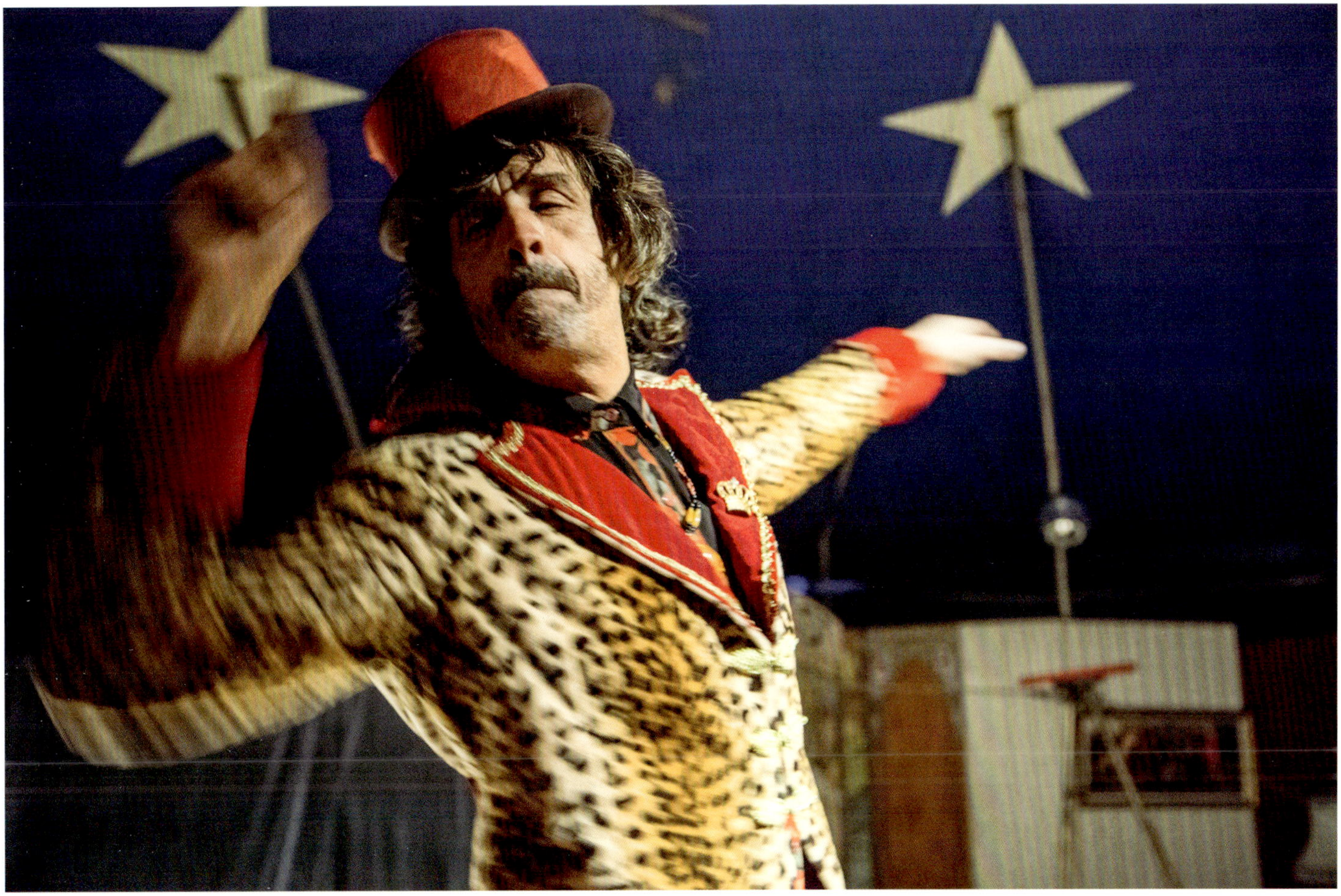

PIGLET CIRCUS
\
Arles – 2014

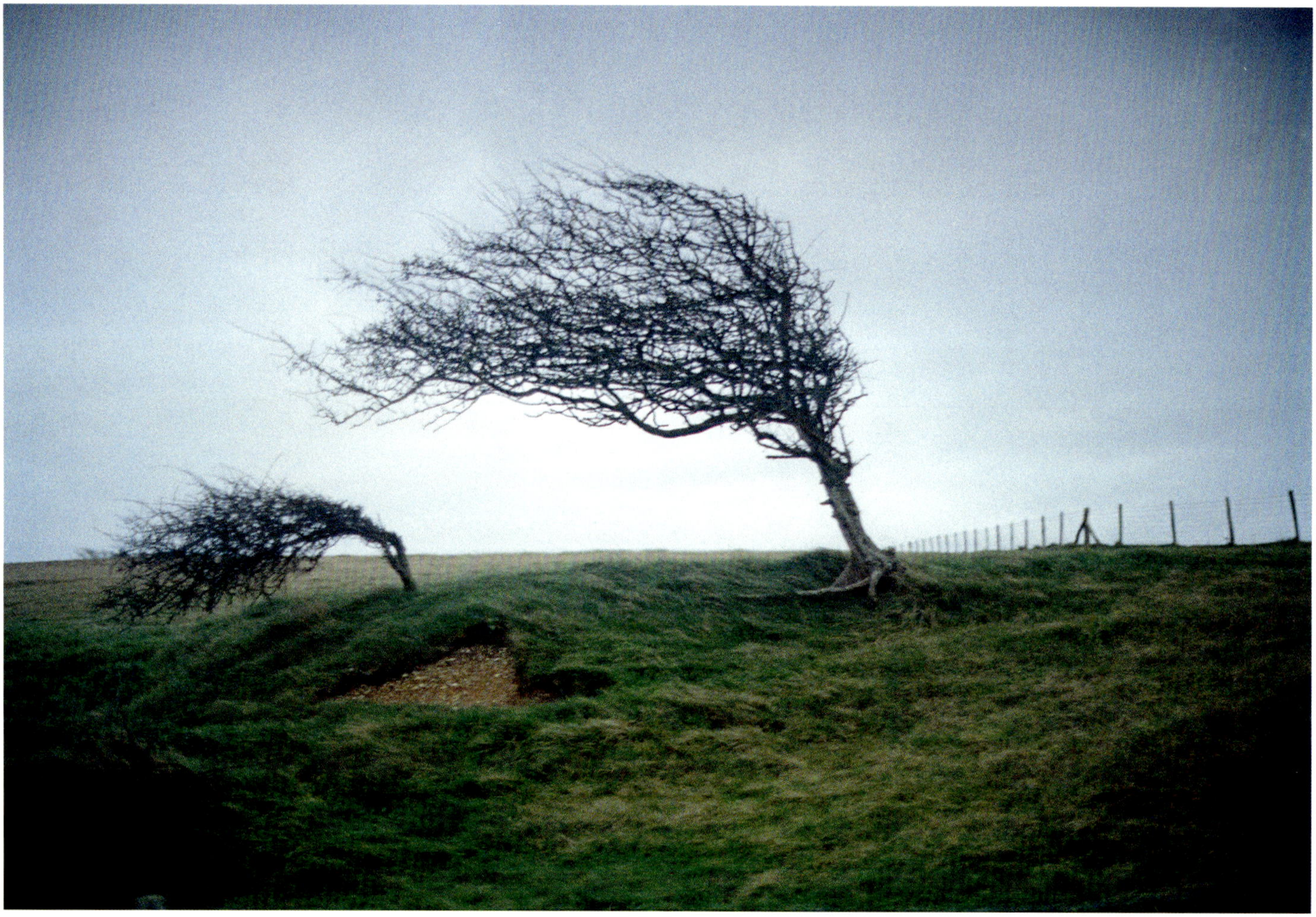

RIVER OUSE VALLEY
\
England – 2008

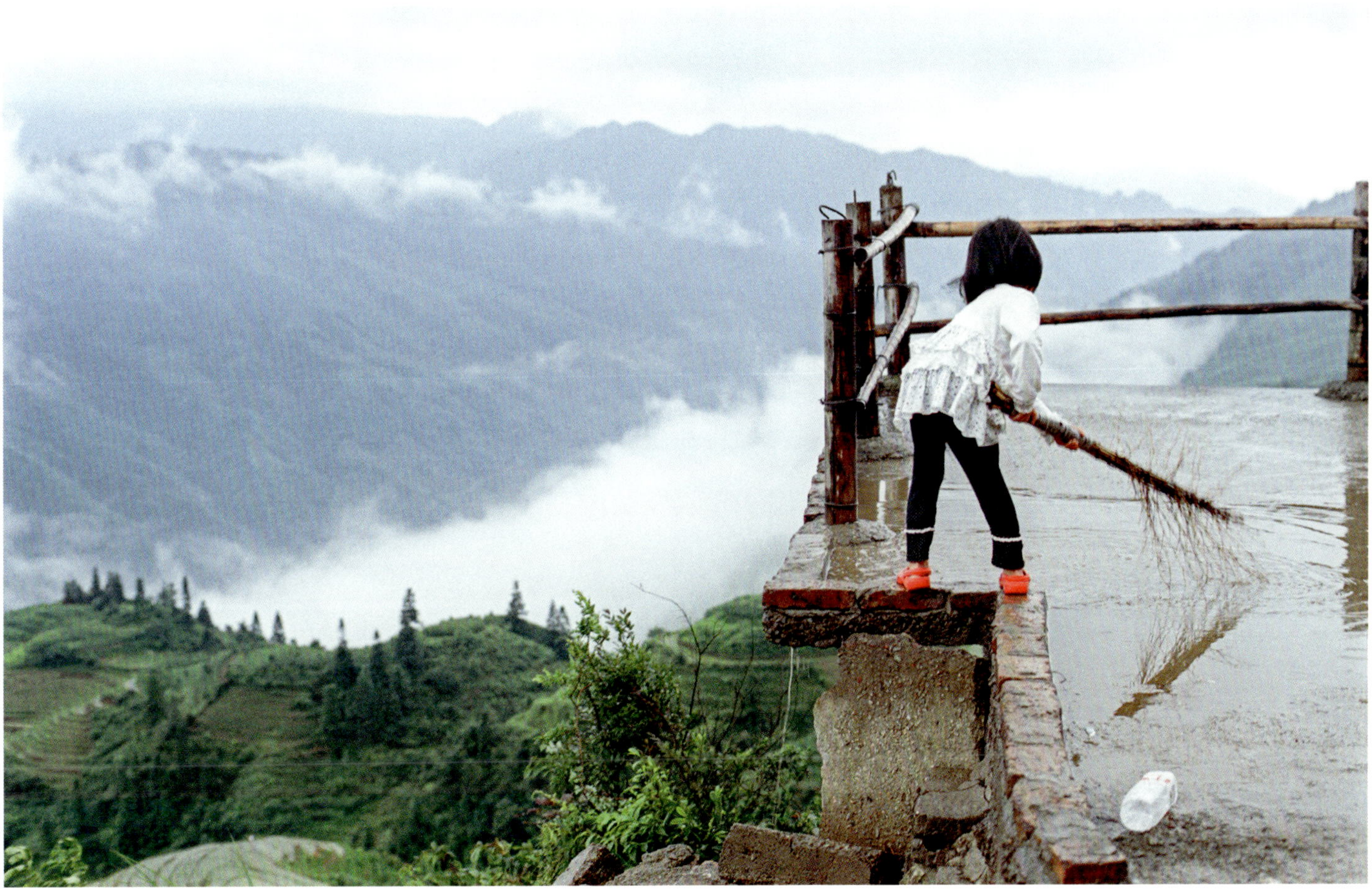

DRAGON'S BACKBONE
\
China – 2009

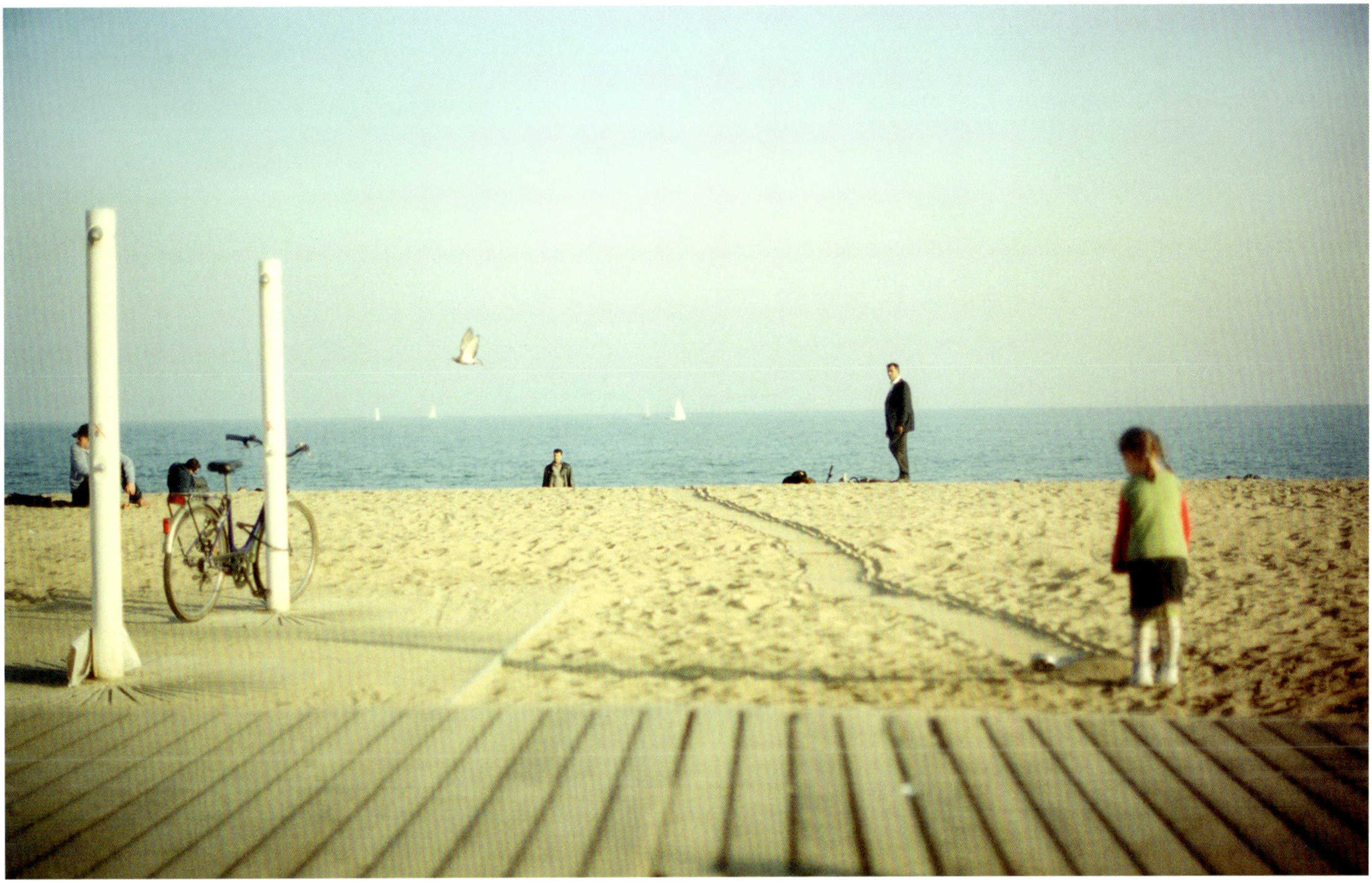

BARCELONETA

\

Spain – 2004

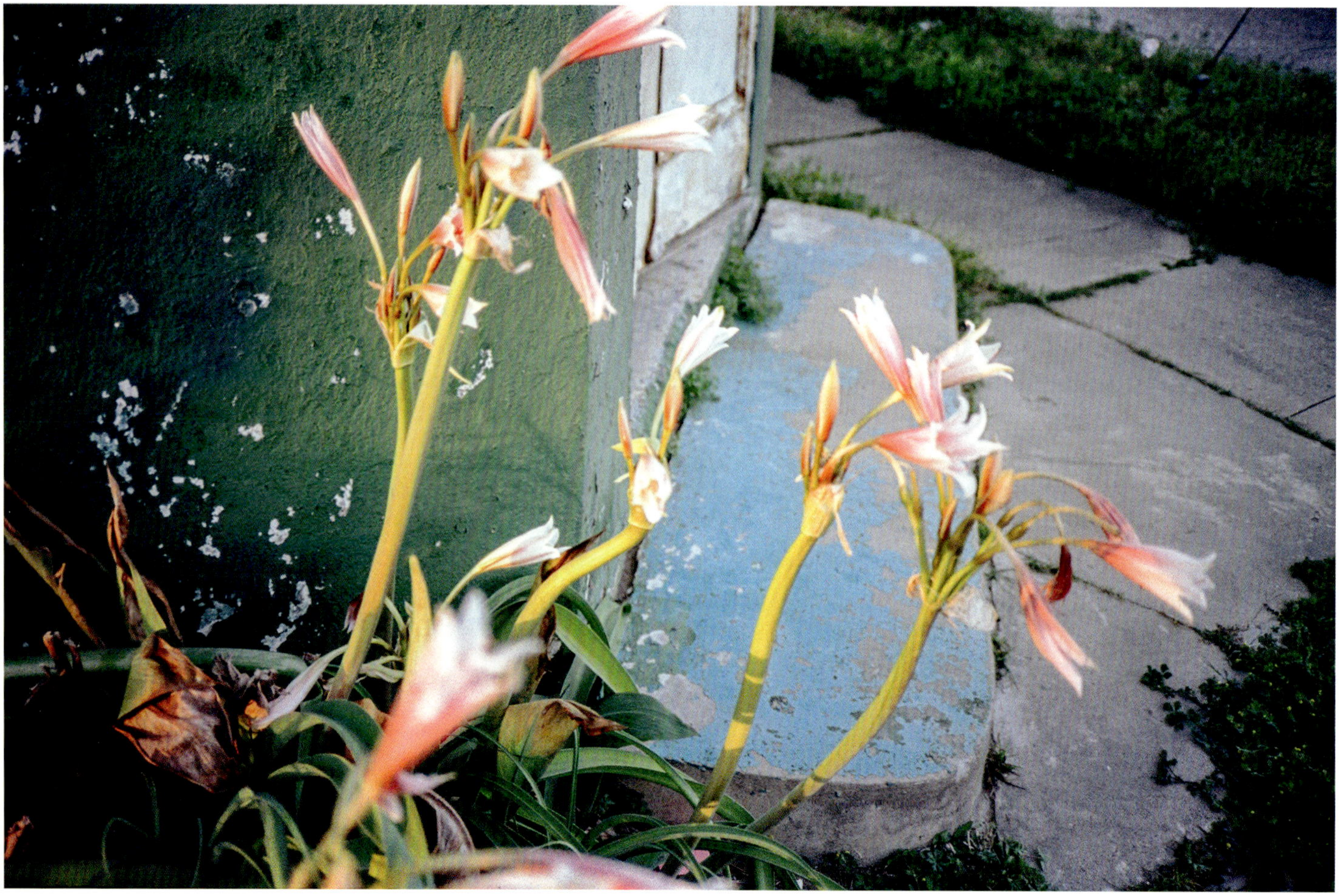

BLUE STOOP

\

Houston – 2002

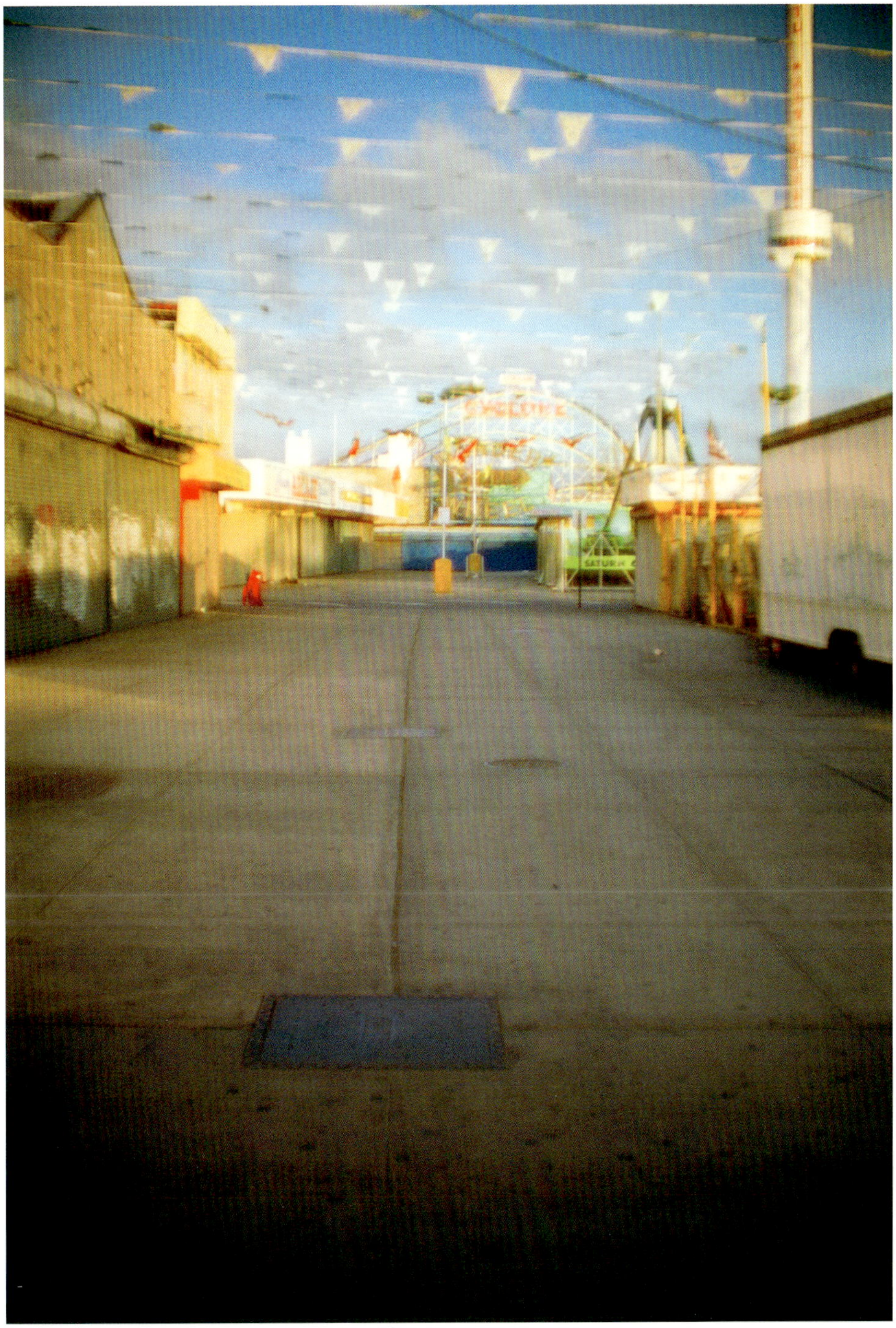

CONEY ISLAND "CLOSED DUE TO TERROR"
\
NYC – 2001

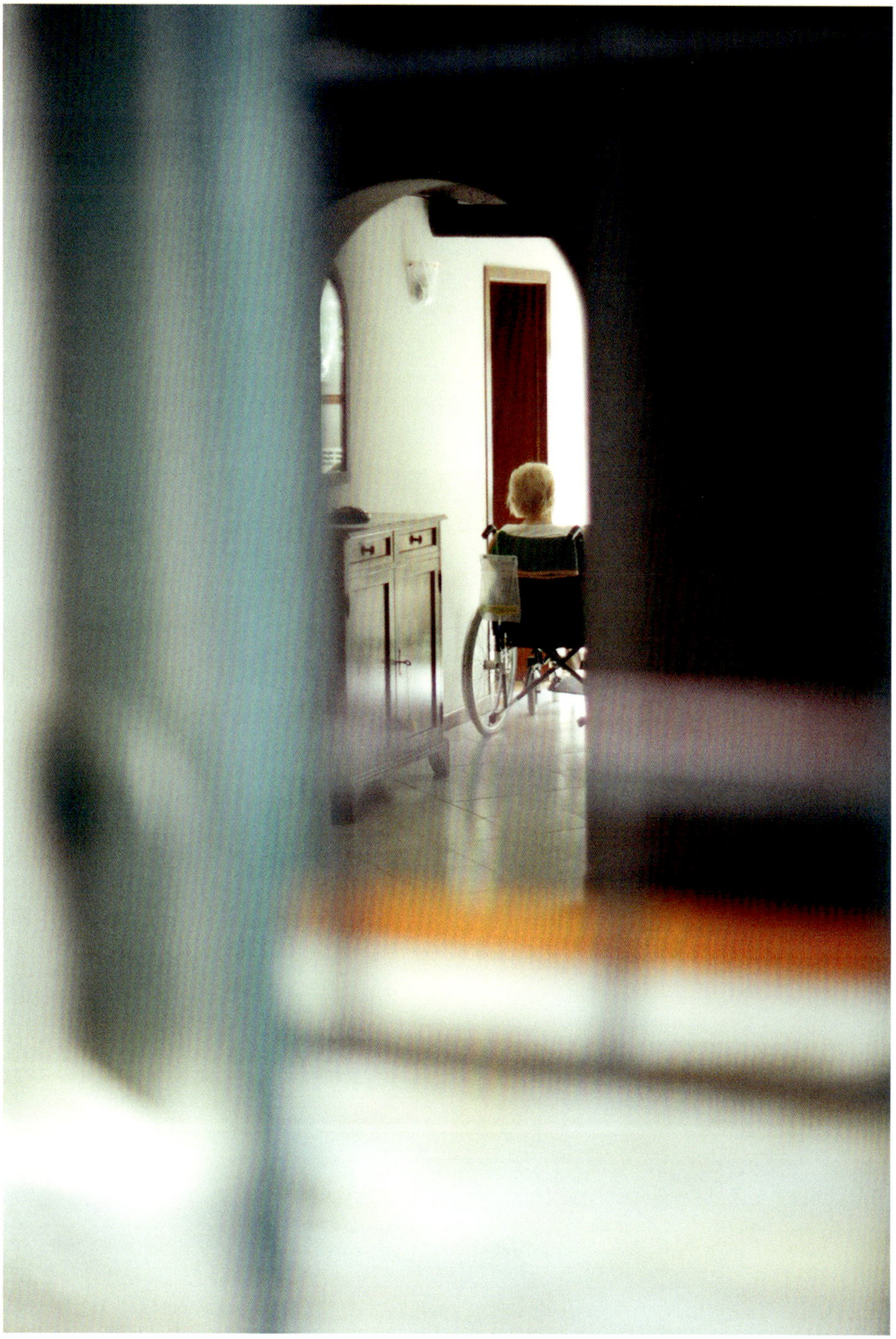

THROUGH A WINDOW

\

Venice – 2003

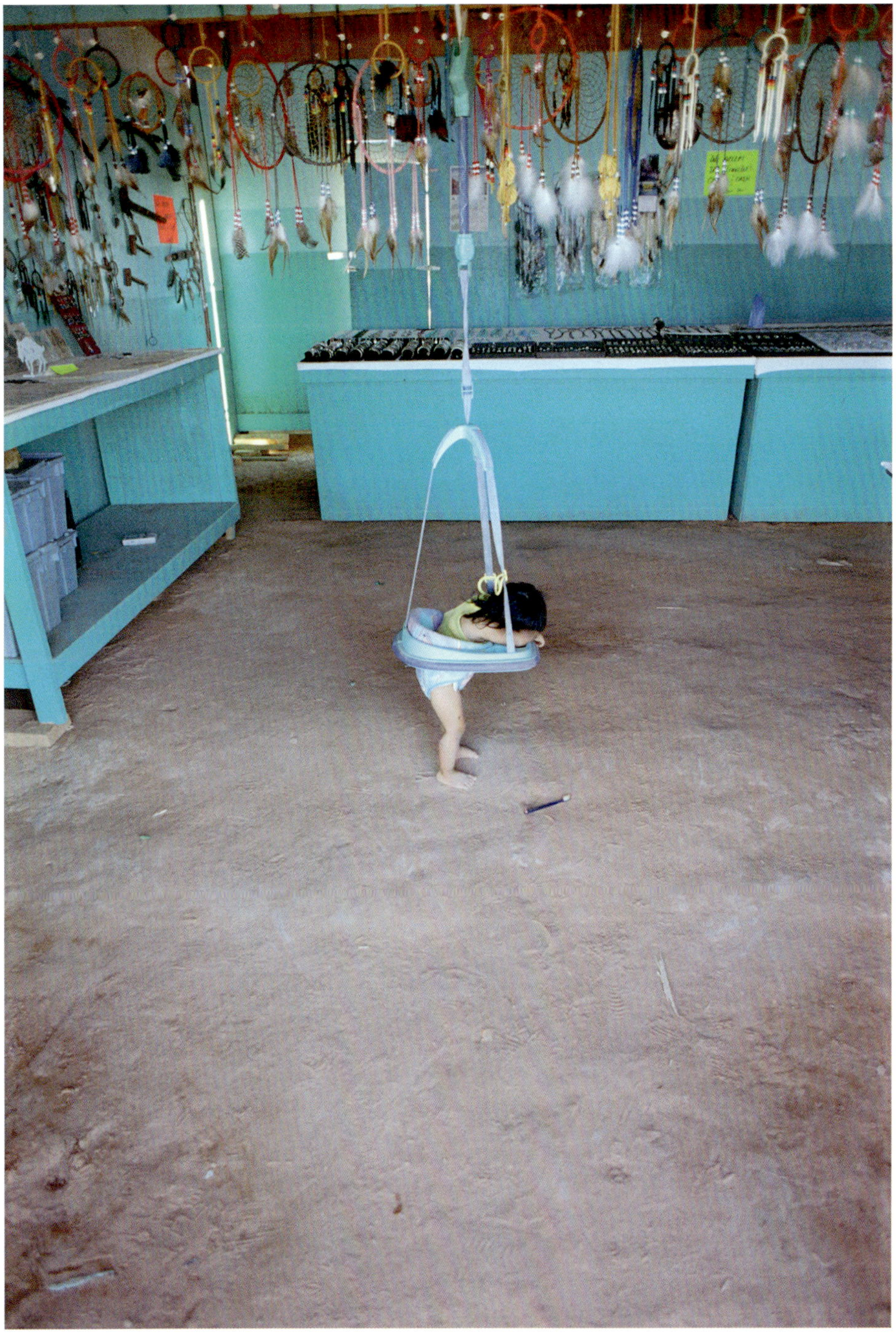

DANGLING NAVAJO CHILD

\

Utah – 1995

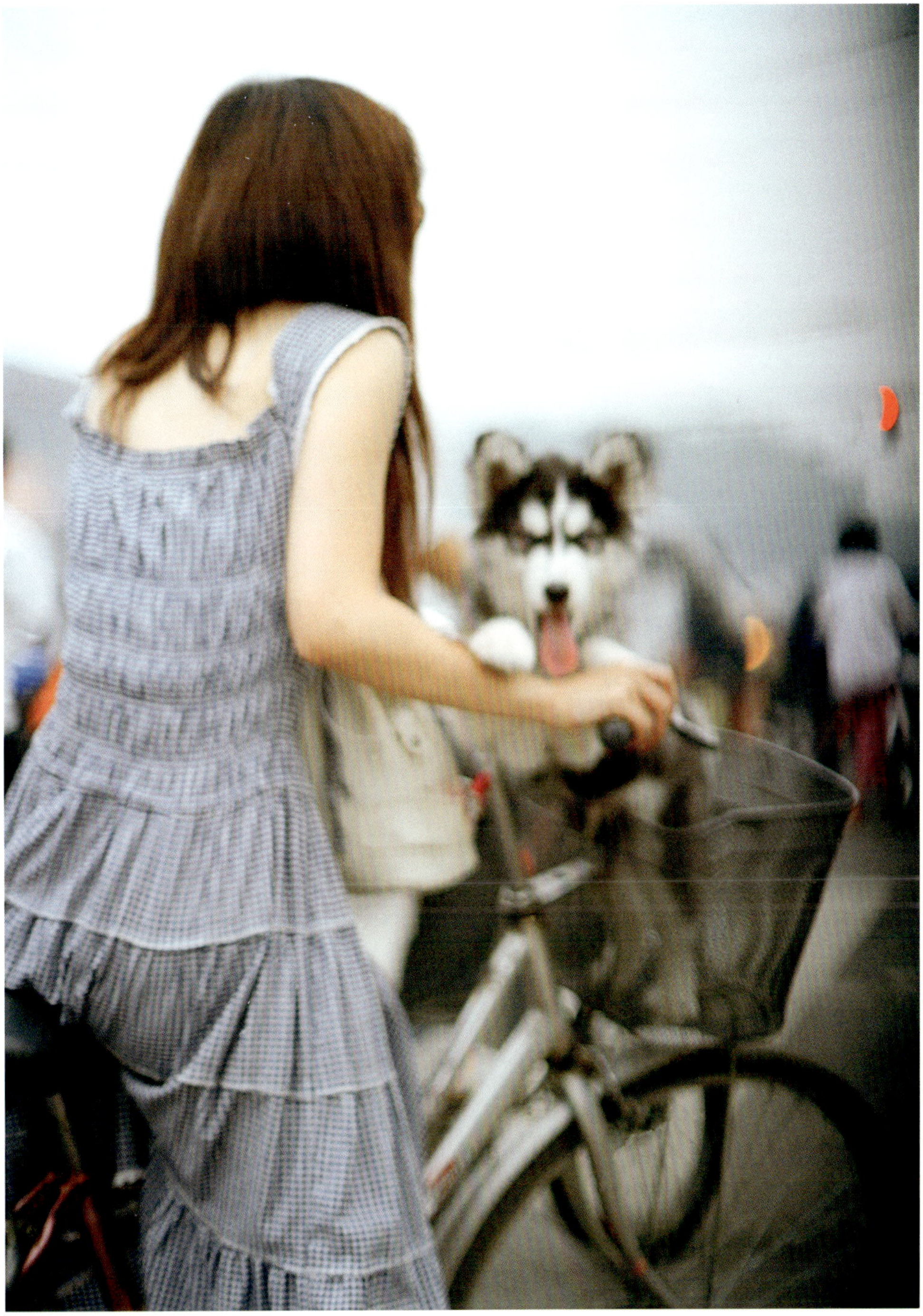

DOG IN BASKET

\

Jaodako, Beijing – 2009

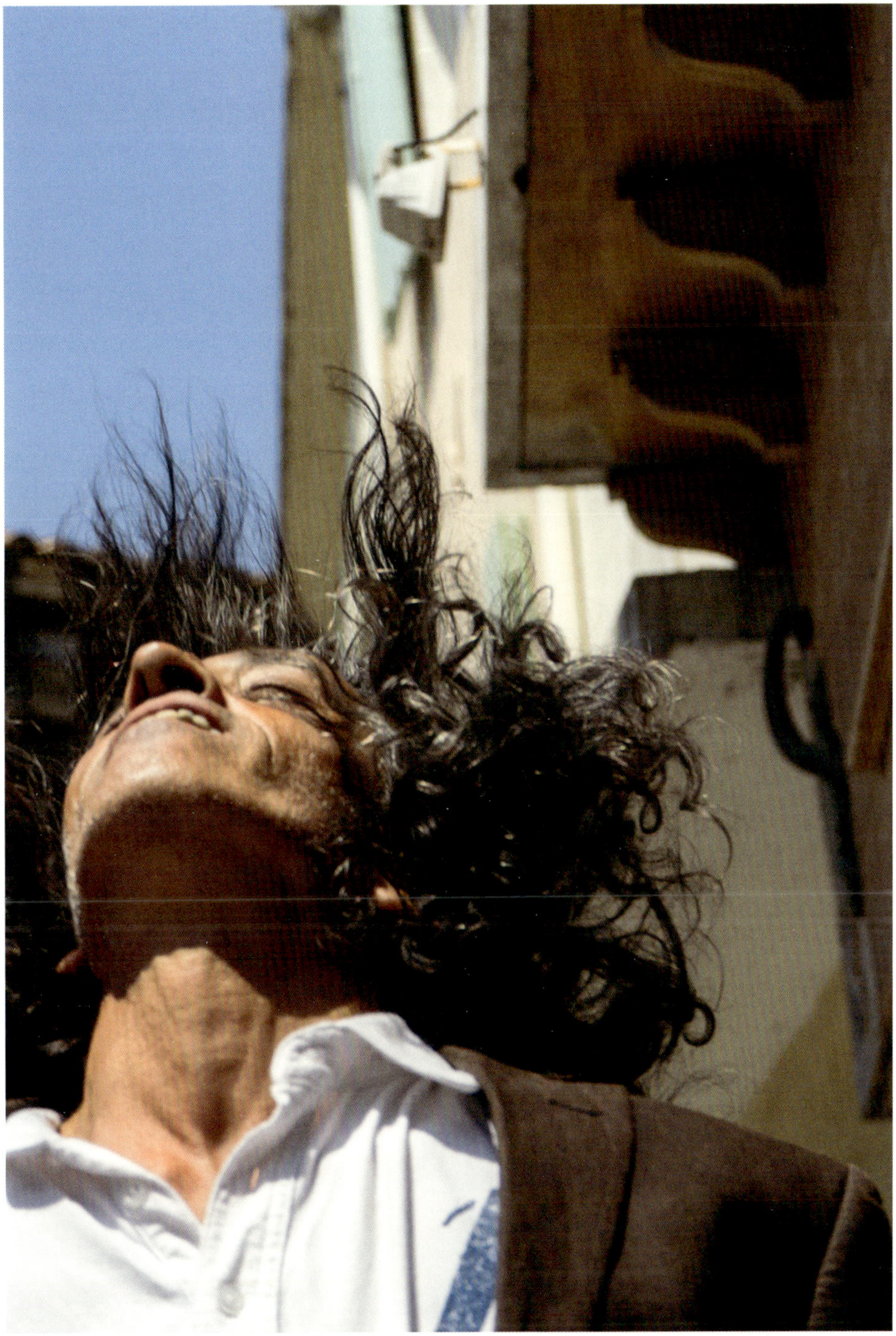

DANCE OF A GITAN
\
Arles – 2013

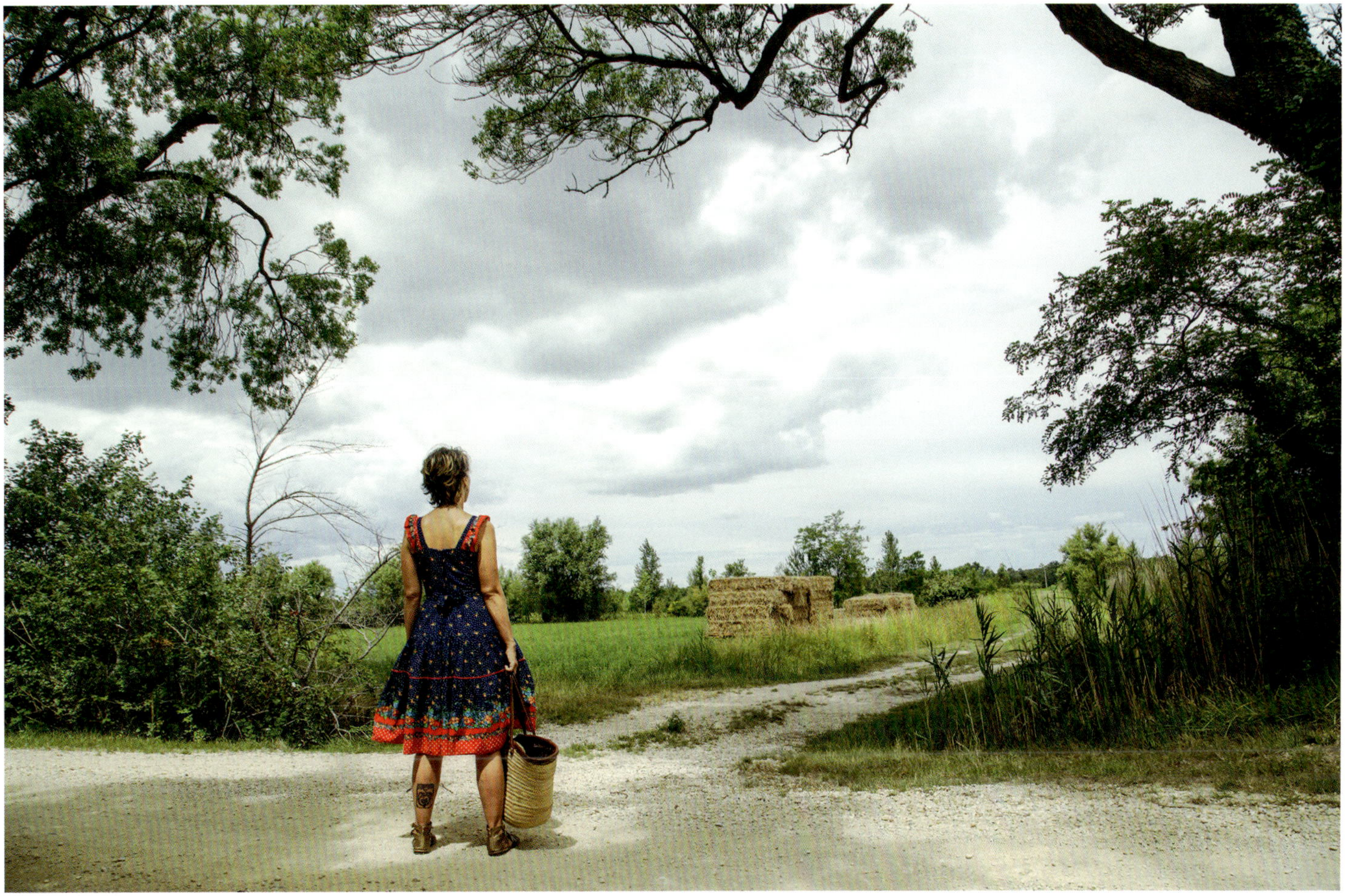

VALENTINE IN THE CAMARGUE

\

2014

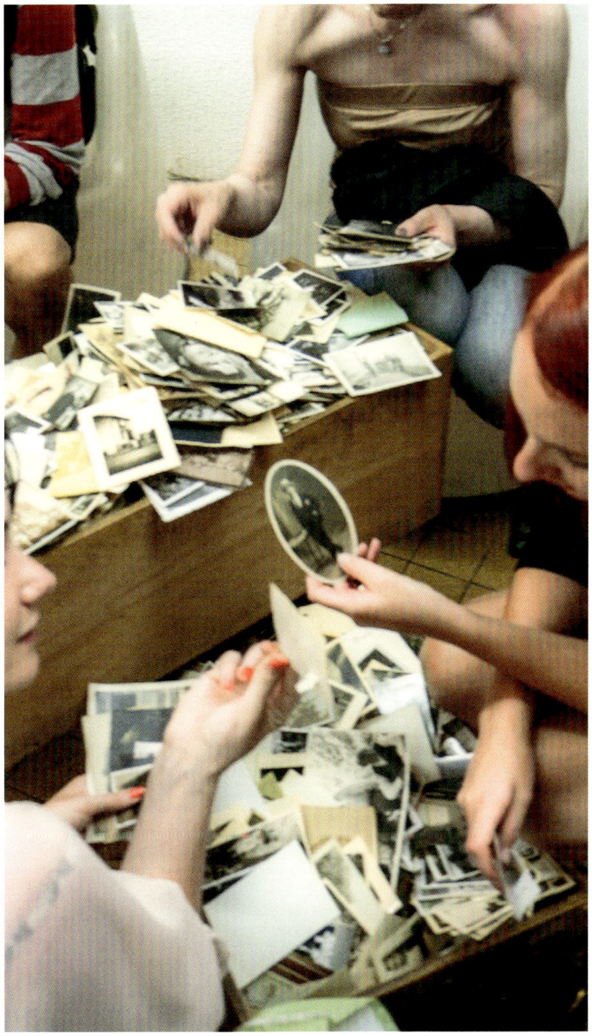

NUIT DE LA ROQUETTE

\

Arles – 2010

no nuttin'

Looking at

David Julian Leonard

\

by W.M. Hunt

Swell title, "Tender is the Light". It is maybe a little arch, but tenderness in photography (and life) is special enough to merit attention. These color photographic works by David Julian Leonard are sweetly sublime. Avoiding rhetorical Southernisms is tricky but these are like real homemade lemonade, more sharp than sweet.

These pictures aren't hectic. They offer the possibility of escape. Release is at hand.

For this photographer, who is also a long time filmmaker and cinematographer, there is no soundtrack. It is all image. It is quiet here, although you might sense someone out of frame quietly humming "I Got Plenty O' Nuttin'".

I don't much like the book's cover. No offense, but little girls in crinoline party dresses? Bleah!

But think birthday party or Valentine's Day. Mr. Leonard's partner is a French lady named Valentine, and everything is dedicated to her. If you ground up those tiny pastel-colored "Be My Valentine" heart shaped ♥ candies and added a little water, you would get a simple color wash with the tint of pink or blue or green. That's what you see here on paper. It's subtle, and it's special.

Proceeding through the book, we quickly get to the boy on the train, looking out the window. We know him. He is more than familiar. He is us. With our collective noses pressed up against the glass, looking out as the train moves on and life races past, we have been here. We are here, forever on our way to New Orleans.

Welcome. It is so swell here. The air moves lightly; it doesn't rain. There are puppies (a great one, a Scottish dog in Sienna) and kitties (Stephen Shore has a cat?) and even bunnies. At some state fair, the artist hunkers down in the midst of a warren of rabbits, with the bunch of bunnies distractedly looking around.

It is heavenly.

Here is many places. Mr. Leonard is the existential traveler. We get Memphis (his home), Arles (his soon to be home), China, Brooklyn, Ireland, Italy, New Orleans. Like that. He's "got plenty o' plenty, hebben the whole day long".

Overwhelmingly, he lives in a world of exalted color. He has the seemingly seamless throwaway skill where colors can be monochromatically lurid (red or green) or color contrasted in an almost calibrated way (blue against yellow, red against green). There is an exceptional talent and eye at work here. "Fog in the Faubourg Marigny, New Orleans, 2007" is a master class lesson in complimentary color.

He has remarked about Charles Miller, whom he refers to as "the great unsung painter of Memphis", "It was Charlie who could better illuminate the pictures with commentary or rhetorical questions. We loved to hear from Charlie because listening to him was like seeing through a prism that refracted light in ways that you couldn't see with your own eyes." This strikes me as true about Leonard's deft handling of color. Like a great musician, he surprises us with how he uniquely finesses the notes.

There is also a manner in which Mr. Leonard wanders through his world – *se balader* in French – easily, unencumbered, pleasantly. It is smarter than describing this as a honeyed Southern lassitude.

The title is a riff on "Tender is the Night" from John Keats' poem "Ode to a Nightingale". Keats' notion of "negative capability" is apt here, a transcendent lack of agenda or compulsive need to make sense, to be able to simply be, to face questions and doubts without always scrambling to make sense of it.

The work is full of empathy. A spare image of a red edged diving board over a dark green rippling pool surface with a peculiarly beckoning light makes one feel a simultaneous yet unfathomable desperation and hope. Leonard truly shares his world and takes you to it. Trust the journey.

The Keats poem continues with "there is no light, save what from heaven is with the breezes blown through verdurous glooms and winding mossy ways", a fine description of how Mr. Leonard sees..."heaven with the breezes blown".

des tout petits riens

Regard sur

David Julian Leonard

\

by W.M. Hunt

Au poil, ce titre, «Tender is the Light.» (Tendre est la lumière). C'est peut-être un peu cliché, mais la tendresse en photographie (et dans la vie) compte assez pour mériter notre attention. Ces œuvres photographiques par David Julian Leonard sont onctueusement sublimes. Eviter la rhétorique sudiste n'est pas facile, mais elles sont comme de la vraie limonade faite maison, plus âpres que sucrées.

Ces images ne sont pas agitées. Elles offrent une échappée. La libération est à portée de main.

Pour ce photographe qui est aussi cinéaste, il n'y a pas de bande son. Tout est image. C'est calme, ici, bien qu'il y ait sans doute quelqu'un, hors-champ, qui fredonne doucement, «I Got Plenty of Nuttin'».

Je n'aime pas beaucoup la couverture. Je ne voudrais pas dire, mais des petites filles en tutu à crinoline! Beurk!

Mais pensez à une fête d'anniversaire ou à la Saint-Valentin. La partenaire de Monsieur Leonard est une dame française qui s'appelle Valentine et tout lui est dédié. Si on broyait ces petits bonbons pastel en forme de coeur ♥ «Be My Valentine» et qu'on y ajoute un peu d'eau, on obtiendrait simplement une teinture rose ou bleue ou verte. C'est ce qu'on trouve ici, sur ce papier, et ça compte.

Plus avant dans le livre, on arrive bientôt au garçon dans le train qui regarde par la fenêtre. On le connaît. Il nous est plus que familier. Il est nous-mêmes. Avec notre nez collectif pressé contre la vitre, regardant au-dehors tandis que le train avance et que la vie se précipite, on est passé par là. On est bien là, perpétuellement en route pour la Nouvelle Orléans.

Bienvenue. C'est parfait, ici. L'air remue doucement; il ne pleut pas. Il y a des petits chiens (un génial chien écossais à Sienne) et des petits chats (Stephen Shore a-t-il un chat?) et même des petits lapins. À une fête foraine, l'artiste s'accroupit au milieu d'un terrier et distraitement, les bestioles regardent ce qui se passe autour.

C'est le paradis.

Ici, c'est plein d'endroits. Monsieur Leonard est un voyageur existentiel. On y trouve Memphis (chez lui), Arles (bientôt chez lui), la Chine, Brooklyn, l'Irlande, l'Italie, la Nouvelle Orléans. Rien que ça. Il «got plenty o' plenty, hebben the whole day long».

Il vit principalement dans un monde aux couleurs exaltées. Il possède cette capacité, en apparence facile et naturelle, selon laquelle les couleurs peuvent être monochromatiquement criardes (rouge ou vert) ou bien en contrastes calibrés (bleu contre jaune, rouge contre vert). Il y a ici un talent et un regard exceptionnels. «Brouillard sur le Faubourg Marigny, New Orleans, 2007») est un cours magistral en couleurs complémentaires.

À propos de Charlie Miller, qu'il considère comme «le grand peintre méconnu de Memphis,» il dit: «C'était Charlie qui savait le mieux illuminer les tableaux avec ses commentaires ou ses questions. On adorait écouter Charlie, parce que l'écouter c'était comme regarder à travers un prisme qui réfracte la lumière d'une manière qu'on n'aurait jamais vue avec nos yeux propres.» C'est vrai aussi de l'habileté que montre Leonard avec la couleur. Comme un grand musicien, il nous surprend par la finesse inimitable avec laquelle il joue les notes.

Il y a aussi une manière qu'a Leonard de se promener dans son monde. Il se balade sans gêne, avec aise et légèreté. C'est plus élégant que de dire mielleuse lassitude sudiste.

Le titre est une variation sur le thème «Tender is the Night» («Tendre est la nuit»), du poème de John Keats, «Ode à un rossignol». L'idée de Keats de «capacité négative» est ici de rigueur: absence transcendantale d'agenda ou du besoin compulsif de donner du sens; simple capacité à être, à faire face aux questions et aux doutes sans toujours s'épuiser à essayer de comprendre.

L'œuvre est remplie d'empathie. L'image dépouillée d'un plongeoir au contour rouge au-dessus d'une piscine ondulante vert sombre avec une lumière particulièrement alléchante nous fait nous sentir, incompréhensiblement, à la fois désespérés et pleins d'espoir. Leonard partage réellement son univers et vous y amène. Laissez-vous porter.

Le poème de Keats continue avec, «Pourtant ici nulle lumière, / Sinon ce qui nous vient des cieux avec les brises / Et court sur les chemins moussus ...» — belle description de ce que voit M. Leonard, «ce qui nous vient des cieux avec les brises.»

ACKNOWLEDGMENT

\ Much gratitude to W.M. – Bill – Hunt for so eloquently saying with his words what I've meant to show through these pictures \ To Valentine Leonard for her brilliant appreciation of the creative process and her honest insights along the way \ ArtsMemphis and Nikii Richey, who curated an exhibition at just the right time to find some final image selections \ Curators and friends Lee Askew, Beate Cegielska, Charlotte Cotton, Mic and Henri Moulard, Rui Prata, Amber Roome, and Liz Smith for helping create opportunities to exhibit over the years \ Collectors and other friends and family whose support and insights have carried me further along include Joachim Paiva, Marianne Leonard, Banks and Anne Leonard, Sara and Frosty Lovitt, Cécile Moulard, P.H. Moulard and Laura Schneegans, Iddo Patt, Stanton Thomas, Peggy Turley, and the late Dr. Roy Tyrer \ David Williams at the Edinburgh College of Art and David Horan at the University of Memphis allowed access to color labs where I learned to print in the dark \ Loulou Williams showed me things I needed to show \ Marla Sweeney led me to places I wouldn't have known to go \ Alexa Becker, Erik Klewe, Shiva Hamid, Loreen Lampe and the Kehrer crew provided excellent support and collaboration in the creation of the book \ William Eggleston has for many years offered encouragement, support and friendship. The influence of his uncompromising vision is immeasurable \ The late Charles Miller is another Memphis artist and friend who taught me how to see \And I am most grateful to everyone who shares their responses to my work. I continue to learn about what I have shown through your eyes.

REMERCIEMENTS

\ Immense gratitude à W.M. Bill Hunt pour avoir su si bien dire avec ses mots ce que j'ai voulu dire avec ces photos \ À Valentine Leonard pour sa brillante compréhension du processus créatif et sa vision pénétrante \ À ArtsMemphis et Nikii Richey, qui a organisé une exposition au moment clé, qui m'a permis de faire cette sélection d'images \ À mes amis et conservateurs Lee Askew, Beate Cegielska, Charlotte Cotton, Mic and Henri Moulard, Rui Prata, Amber Roome, et Liz Smith pour avoir su créer des opportunités d'exposition \ Les collectionneurs, famille et amis dont le soutien et les idées m'ont permis d'avancer: Joachim Paiva, Marianne Leonard, Banks and Anne Leonard, Sara and Frosty Lovitt, Cécile Moulard, P.H. Moulard and Laura Schneegans, Iddo Patt, Stanton Thomas, Peggy Turley, et feu Dr. Roy Tyrer \ David Williams au Edinburgh College of Art et David Horan à l'université de Memphis m'ont permis l'accès aux laboratoires couleurs où j'ai appris à imprimer dans le noir \ Loulou Williams m'a montré des choses que je devais montrer \ Marla Sweeney m'a mené à des endroits où je n'aurais pas su aller \ Alexa Becker, Erik Klewe, Shiva Hamid, Loreen Lampe et l'équipe de Kehrer m'ont apporté un soutien et une collaboration excellents pour la création de ce livre \ William Eggleston m'a pendant des années apporté encouragement, soutien et amitié. L'influence de sa vision sans compromis est incalculable \ Feu Charles Miller est un autre artiste et ami cher de Memphis qui m'a appris à voir \ Et je suis surtout reconnaissant à tous ceux qui partagent leurs réactions à mon travail. C'est par leur regard que je continue à apprendre ce que j'ai montré.

DAVID JULIAN LEONARD

\ born – Memphis 1962 \ **zodiac sign** – Gemini with moon and two other houses in Taurus \ **education** – dropped out of school – learned best by life experience – studied photography at elbow of Bill Eggleston \ **personal dictum** – "the average of all of us is the enemy of each of us." \ **married** to Valentine Leonard a French philosopher, writer, musician and yoga teacher \ **residence** – together they share houses in Memphis and Arles

AS PHOTOGRAPHER

\ **solo exhibitions** include: The Photographers' Gallery – London (1999), Åarhus Kunstbygning – Åarhus, Denmark (2003), Museu da Imagem – Braga, Portugal (2004), Amber Roome Contemporary Arts – Edinburgh (2006), La Maison sur la Place – Senlis, France (2007), ArtsMemphis Gallery (2015) \ **public collections** include: Austin Museum of Art – Texas, Memphis Brooks Museum of Art – Tennessee, Musée de la Photographie à Charleroi – Belgium, Museum of Modern Art – Rio De Janeiro, New Orleans Museum of Art – Louisiana, Ogden Museum of Southern Art – New Orleans, Scottish National Photography Collection / National Portrait Gallery – Edinburgh, Telfair Museum of Art – Savannah, Georgia \ **private collections** include: The Berman Collection – Los Angeles, Francis Coppola – San Francisco, William Eggleston – Memphis, W.M. Hunt – New York, Joaquim Paiva – Brasilia

AS FILMMAKER

\ **cinematographer** on documentaries including: *Best of Enemies, Respect Yourself: The Stax Records Story, Johnny Cash's America,* and *The Big Beat: The Story of Fats Domino & His Band* \ **grip and lighting technician** on feature films including: *The People vs Larry Flynt, The Rainmaker, Cookie's Fortune* \ **actor** played Avery, a teenage car thief, in *Final Chapter: Walking Tall* \ **editor & producer** *Big Star Live in Memphis* \ director of documentaries including – *Why Elvis?* and at time of this publication a film about musician Alex Chilton.

W.M. – BILL – HUNT

is a champion of photography: a collector, curator and consultant who lives and works quietly in New York City. He teaches, writes, organizes projects (*The Unseen Eye: Photographs from the Unconscious*; *Hunt's Three Ring Circus: American Groups Before 1950*) and looks at many pictures.

DAVID JULIAN LEONARD

\ **Né à** Memphis en 1962 \ **Signe astrologique:** Gémeaux avec lune et deux autres maisons en Taureau \ **formation:** lycée - formé à l'experience vécue — a étudié la photographie avec Bill Eggleston \ **Diction personnel:** "la moyenne de tous est l'ennemi de chacun." \ Marié à Valentine Leonard, philosophe, écrivaine, musicienne et professeure de yoga français \ Résidence - le couple partage deux maisons à Arles et Memphis.

PHOTOGRAPHE

\ **Expositions solo**: The Photographers' Gallery - Londres (1999), Åarhus Kunstbygning - Åar- hus, Danmark (2003), Museu da Imagem - Braga, Portugal (2004), Amber Roome Contemporary Arts - Edimbourg (2006), La Maison sur la Place - Senlis, France (2007), ArtsMemphis Gallery (2015) \ **Collections publiques:** Austin Museum of Art - Texas, Memphis Brooks Museum of Art - Tennessee, Musée de la Photographie à Charleroi - Belgique, Museum of Modern Art - Rio De Janeiro, New Orleans Museum of Art - Louisiana, Ogden Museum of Southern Art - New Orleans, Scottish National Photography Collection / National Portrait Gallery - Edinburgh, Telfair Museum of Art - Savannah, Georgia \ **Collections privées:** The Berman Collection - Los Angeles, Francis Coppola - San Francisco, William Eggleston - Memphis, W.M. Hunt - New York, Joaquim Paiva - Brasilia

CINÉASTE

\ **Directeur photo et cameraman** sur des films documentaires: *Best of Enemies, Respect Yourself: The Stax Records Story, Johnny Cash's America,* and *The Big Beat: The Story of Fats Domino & His Band* \ **Machiniste caméra et technicien lumière sur des longs-métrages:** *The People vs Larry Flynt, The Rainmaker, Cookie's Fortune* \ **Acteur:** a joué Avery, un adolescent voleur de voitures dans *Final Chapter: Walking Tall* \ **Montage et production:** *Big Star Live in Memphis* \ *Réalisateur* de films documentaires - *Why Elvis?* Et actuellement en cours: un film sur le musicien Alex Chilton.

W.M. – BILL – HUNT

est un champion de la photographie: collectionneur, commissaire en arts et consultant qui vit et travaille tranquillement à New York. Il enseigne, écrit, organise des expositions (*The Unseen Eye: photographies de l'inconscient*; *Le cirque de Hunt: groupes américains avant 1950*) et regarde beaucoup de photos.

Text \ Texte
W.M. Hunt

Translation \ Traduction
Valentine Leonard

Proofreading \ Correction des épreuves
Elisabeth Buchet-Deák, France Picard

Design \ Maquette
Kehrer Design Heidelberg
(Loreen Lampe, Erik Clewe)

Image processing \ Iconographie
Kehrer Design Heidelberg (Erik Clewe)

Production \ Fabrication
Kehrer Design Heidelberg (Andreas Schubert)

Cover Illustration \ Illustration de couverture
GARDEN PARTY, Memphis – 2001

frontispiece \ frontispice
HOFFMAN ESTATE, THE CAMARGUE,
France – 2002

Printed and bound in Germany
ISBN 978-3-86828-695-3

Kehrer Heidelberg Berlin
www.kehrerverlag.com